TORMENTED
THE ANDY McLAREN STORY

Andy McLaren with Mark Guidi

MAINSTREAM
PUBLISHING

EDINBURGH AND LONDON

This book is dedicated to Claire, Dylan and Tyler.

Thanks for believing in me more than I did, and for always trying to see the good in me. I hope this book goes some way towards explaining the regret I feel about the way I treated you all.

Copyright © Andy McLaren and Mark Guidi, 2007
All rights reserved
The moral rights of the authors have been asserted

First published in Great Britain in 2007 by
MAINSTREAM PUBLISHING COMPANY
(EDINBURGH) LTD
7 Albany Street
Edinburgh EH1 3UG

ISBN 9781845962746

A catalogue record for this book is available
from the British Library

Typeset in Gill Sans and Palatino

Printed in Great Britain by
William Clowes Ltd, Beccles, Suffolk

ACKNOWLEDGEMENTS

I would like to thank Mainstream for publishing *Tormented*, particularly Bill Campbell for showing tremendous belief in the book from our very first meeting. To Graeme Blaikie and Paul Murphy for their excellent work, and patience and understanding as I missed deadline after deadline. To my mum and dad, brothers John and Jamie and sister Denise, and to Claire's family – thanks for being there when I was in need of help and for putting up with me. To my mum's family, the Lappins, especially old Lizzie – they all know how much they mean to me. To Angela Maguire, AA and the Priory for saving my life. To the English PFA for helping me get my life back on track. To Ally McCoist for the foreword and telling lies about me in it, making me out to be a good guy. To the managers, coaches and players for telling it as it is about me in this book – appreciated. To Derek McInnes for being a special pal. And to all my pals out there – there are just too many of you to mention. To John Viola and Dave McGhie – thanks for standing by me and being there. To Doc McGuinness and Peter Kay for sorting me out at the right time. Unfortunately, a few friends will not get the chance to read this as they've been taken early from us in tragic circumstances – you will always be in my thoughts. To Mark Guidi for his excellent work in putting my thoughts into words and never placing me or my family under pressure. To Brian McSweeney at the *Sunday Mail* for his major input and patience.

And to the rest of the staff at the *Sunday Mail* sports desk for various degrees of input. Also to David McKie for casting his eye over it. Finally, thanks to Jeff Holmes for talking me into taking my top off for the cover photo!

Mark Guidi would like to thank Claire, Angela Maguire, Derek McInnes and John McLaren – they know why. Much appreciation to Brian McSweeney for his support and time. Thanks to the various people who gave up their time to contribute to this book. Thanks to Bill, Graeme and Paul at Mainstream for making this as smooth an operation as possible, and to Andy for selecting me to work with him on his book.

CONTENTS

Foreword

ANDY MCLAREN'S drinking problems are well documented. But the first thing I have to say is that I'd like Craig Brown to be breathalysed for having given Andy a Scotland cap. Still, that opportunity to play against Poland has made Andy unique in international footballing terms. He achieved the impossible by getting two caps in one night: his first and last!

On a more serious note, I'm delighted to be given the opportunity to write the foreword for his book. I worked with Andy at Kilmarnock but, prior to that, played against him many times during my career with Rangers. What I remember about him was that he was mouthy on the pitch but, unlike some, had the ability to back up his cheek. His own teammates would get it from him, as would his opponents. He was the original wee upstart.

We then became teammates at Rugby Park when he joined the club just three or four months after admitting to being an alcoholic. He came into the fold at Kilmarnock and never tried to pretend he was something he wasn't. He was honest and open about the problems he had faced. He would often tell stories about what he'd got up to in the past and explain that he'd never led his life in as professional a manner as he should have. The younger professionals listened. And, more importantly, they learned. It was a great education for them and must have been therapeutic for

Andy. There's no doubt he has had experiences in life that young players up and down the country could benefit from in terms of learning the potential pitfalls of drug and alcohol abuse.

The older guys, myself included, also took great interest in what Andy had to say. Some of his stories were serious and brought a look of disbelief to my face. Some stories also brought a smile. My goodness, when I think back to what he told us back then and what he says in this book, he makes Keith Richards look like he's led the life of Aled Jones!

Andy was going through a recovery process during those early months at Rugby Park, and I reckon the brilliant characters we had in the dressing-room at the time helped him through it. He'd travel to training in a car with Mark Reilly, Ally Mitchell and Paul Wright, and that must have helped him. All three were clued up and good professionals.

Then, when he arrived for training, he'd have a total contrast with me and Durranty to contend with! I thought the best way to deal with Andy when he first came to Killie was with as much humour as possible. There was no point in tiptoeing around him and pretending that he had lived the life of an angel. I'm not one for glossing over things. Trying to lighten things up is a great way of getting things into the open and breaking the ice. It doesn't mean you don't care or lack sensitivity. I knew Andy was from Castlemilk in Glasgow and that he would respond positively to a sense of humour.

So, when he missed a great chance in training or on a match day, I'd look over at him and say, 'Hey, the sooner you get back on the booze, the better!' Andy would laugh and tell me to shut my fat face. There was no hiding place at Kilmarnock, whether you were a young pro or a more experienced campaigner, such as Gus MacPherson, Kevin McGowne or Gordon Marshall. You dished it out and you took it back. It's what makes a good dressing-room and helps build a great team spirit. And we had that at Killie.

Having fun was encouraged by Bobby Williamson, Gerry McCabe and Jim Clark. They were the gaffers but enjoyed a laugh with the players. Their management style worked, because Kilmarnock qualified for Europe four seasons out of the five that Bobby and his staff were in charge. So, Kilmarnock was the perfect club for Andy to join at that stage of his life. And he played some of the finest football of his career, which totally justified his decision to turn down other clubs.

I'm just glad Andy has managed to come through the other side. From his childhood through to his late 20s, he's had to deal with things you wouldn't wish on your worst enemy. I'm pleased to say his problems are behind him and he is doing well.

There must be people he has to thank for his recovery, but I'm sure no one more so than his good lady Claire. She deserves a medal for standing by Andy and keeping their family together. It couldn't have been easy for her during those dark days. There's no doubt she is an exceptional woman. And credit to their sons Dylan and Tyler for helping their mum cope with the stress and pressure she must have been under. And the kids being there must have given Andy the will to live when he was at his lowest ebb.

He made the headlines many times, quite often for the wrong reasons. However, what shouldn't be overlooked is his contribution as a footballer. From my own experience as his teammate, he had wonderful ability and bravery. He was also a terrific lad to have in the dressing-room. Few could put up with Durranty and me when we were in full flow, but Andy was rarely left behind.

It was also a credit to him that he took part in every social event organised by the boys. He never missed a night out and was the life and soul. It would have been easier for him to stay in for a quiet night and not surround himself with boys having a drink, particularly as he was still in the early stages of his recovery. But he stood up to every challenge and never once asked the boys to make allowances for him. As long as we were having fun, Andy was happy. He'd have hated it to be any other way.

The biggest compliment I can pay him is that he made people smile. When I think of Andy McLaren, happy memories spring to mind, and you can't say that about too many people.

Ally McCoist MBE
October 2007

I

DRIVEN TO DESTRUCTION

IT WAS April 2006. I'd been on a downer for months. I woke up one morning and wasn't in a good mood. I'd had yet another argument with my partner Claire the night before. We woke up not talking to one another. It's true what they say about never going to sleep on bad terms. She was going to visit friends in Edinburgh that day, and I drove her through in the morning. Needless to say, the atmosphere between us was frosty and hardly a word was spoken, although I wouldn't have heard her even if she had been saying anything to me, as I was so engrossed in my own thoughts.

It was going through my mind to kill myself.

I was crying on the way home from Edinburgh, and I thought I couldn't handle life any more. I'd stopped going to AA (Alcoholics Anonymous) meetings. I tried to convince myself that I was too tired to go, what with all the travelling to work every day and to away games with Morton. Spineless excuses, the lot. The truth was that I had fallen out with myself: didn't want to look in the mirror; didn't think I had a bone in my body worth keeping.

I'd felt this way before – that everybody was sick of me and I was only bringing misery into their lives. Not that anyone had ever said as much to me, and I know my feelings were unfounded, but I'd convinced myself nobody gave a damn about me. So, my solution to the problem was to end it all. From the outside, I know people must have thought that I had nothing to be depressed about. Here I was being paid decent money to be a footballer and with a family that were happy and healthy. Well, healthy, at least. However, on the inside I was in a total state.

I'd thought about killing myself before, but the thoughts I had that morning were the strongest I'd ever felt. In the couple of weeks building up to that day, I looked into ways of making sure Claire and the boys would be taken care of financially. I knew I had to make my death look like an accident, otherwise there would be no pay-outs. In accidental circumstances, the mortgage would be paid off and the English PFA would make a pay-out of around £250,000, because I was still one of their members, although that only applied up until the age of 35. So, the least I could do for my family was to kill myself but not make it look deliberate. It was in my head that they'd be happy if I was gone as long as they were financially secure. I felt as though I was dragging them down with me, holding them back from progressing in life.

I sat on my own one night and made a list of the possible ways to go. I thought about jumping off a building, but I'm scared of heights. Hanging myself was scored off because I didn't know how to tie a noose. I considered overdosing on paracetamol, but I looked into that and found out it could take five days to die, and I didn't want a slow death. And if I managed to come through the overdose, I didn't want to have any sympathy and people saying, 'Poor Andy.'

So, having a car smash and making it look like an accident seemed the best way forward for all concerned. I thought it would be quick and painless. I dropped Claire off in Edinburgh and decided on the way back that I was going to do it. I was motoring along, in auto-pilot fashion, at about 80 miles per hour and had chosen my 'victim'. There was a massive lorry alongside me, the type with huge wheels and a luminous 'Long Vehicle' sign, and I thought that it would be perfect to go into. Belting along the motorway at that speed, I thought I'd have no chance of survival.

I just wanted to drive under its wheels and be smashed to a pulp. I felt as though I'd had a shite life and fuck everybody else.

It was so selfish, not just because I'd be taking my own life away from Claire and my sons, but I could have caused a pile-up on the motorway and other people might have lost their lives. God, innocent people. Someone's mother, someone's father, someone's daughter or someone's son. I was so stupid – so inconsiderate. Twice, my legs went for it, pressing down on the accelerator to batter my car into the lorry, but my arms wouldn't turn the steering wheel. I tried twice and my legs didn't fail me. Thankfully, thinking about it now, my arms did.

I was angry with myself for not being able to go through with it. So, it was in my mind to try a third attempt. I was still on the M8, passing Livingston. I remember that it was catching sight of The Pyramids at the side of the road that made me think twice. A couple of years earlier, I had been on that same road with Tyler, my youngest son. It was just the two of us in the car, the music was blaring and we were having a good laugh together. We were driving past Livingston, and I remember winding up Tyler by telling him that they were the pyramids where the Teletubbies lived. Tyler wasn't sure if I was serious or not, but it was fun thinking of Tinky Winky, Dipsy, Laa-Laa and Po. *Teletubbies* was his favourite programme, and he was happy at the thought that he was close to where they lived. It seems strange to be saying this, but thank God for the Teletubbies. I might not be here had it not been for them.

Thinking of those good times with Tyler brought me back to my senses. I thought of the fun I'd had with him that day and how by killing myself I was going to give all of that up. I didn't want to miss out on those kind of moments, and my boys most definitely did not deserve to lose their dad. My own dad died when I was just 16, and I know how that felt. My boys were younger than that and didn't need me to put them through any more pain than I already had during my days of serious drinking. I'd no right to be thinking about suicide. God, apart from anything else, I hadn't even said a proper goodbye to them or Claire – hadn't kissed them that day or given them a hug. I took myself into my imaginary office and administered a right good talking to. I was being selfish and stupid and had to address my problems and confront them head on, rather than ignore them and pretend everything was hunky-dory.

I drove back to Glasgow and headed to Kings Park. I was emotionally drained and tired. I fell asleep for about four hours in the car. I must have slept until about five in the afternoon.

When I woke up, I knew I had to get back to my AA meetings and sort myself out. I looked upon it as my last chance, and I wasn't going to throw it away. I'd had some really good times in my life, and I wanted to experience them again. I also wanted Claire to see the best of me and my boys to love being with their dad. However, I was a long way off being in that happy state of mind, because, at that moment in time, I was basically fucked. And I had been that way for a few months.

In the past, when I was feeling low I would turn to drink to make me feel good again. It was amazing the number of problems that would disappear after drinking about 20 bottles of Budweiser – or so I thought. However, alcohol wasn't an option for me any more.

Suicide must have first entered my head when I was in my early 20s, usually after I'd come off a heavy booze binge or Claire had packed her bags and moved back down to Glasgow from Dundee because she'd had enough of being let down by me. I'd be depressed coming off the drink and I'd have passing thoughts to take my own life, although it never reached the stage I found myself at in April 2006 when I came one turn of my steering wheel away from putting myself in an early grave.

Old Chris, a good friend of mine from AA who is sadly dead now, used to say that the worst company in the world is an alcoholic on his own, trying to give himself advice. More often than not, the thoughts in your head are negative, and it's important to get people around you as quickly as possible. That's why the AA meetings are so good – they give much-needed comfort. Talking to people makes all the difference – saying it all out loud and then having people there for you to tell you things are not as bad as they seem. Because people in AA helped me to cope with my addiction to alcohol, I had the confidence to take aside two guys whom I trust and tell them about 'IT'.

What is IT? Without knowing it at the time, IT was something that happened to me during my childhood that was to have a more deep-seated impact on my life than I'd ever have guessed, something I've carried since it happened, buried deep inside, and something I've had to think long and hard about revealing in this book.

Anyway, I explained to the guys from AA what I had gone through and what I was still going through. I had carried guilt, anger, frustration and hate around with me for about 25 years, and I had to do something about it. They listened and were really good about it, although they were probably a touch shocked. They gave me sound advice and told me to seek professional help, as this was something that could not be dealt with directly by AA.

In my darkest moments, IT would come back to me. But I tried to bury my feelings away. In my head, I'd dig a hole in the ground, throw IT in there, and then fill it all in again. And again. And again. For long spells, things would be fine, but then IT would resurrect itself and return to haunt me, trying to ruin my life. I knew it was a serious matter and that I had to unburden myself. But rather than take on board the advice given to me by the two lads in AA, I crawled into a shell and never went back to the meetings. That was in about November 2005. I felt embarrassed about what I had told them – and about what had happened to me – and thought that they would never look at me the same way again. I had got it into my mind that they would be laughing at me. God, it's bad enough being an alcoholic, but there's not much chance for you when you are a paranoid one.

Before that, I usually went to three meetings a week. I was going through step four again, which is basically writing down your life story. When I'd previously tackled step four, about four years earlier, I never made any reference to IT, because I didn't think I needed to, even though it was the one big thing I had to confront and get into the open. I struggled to put it on paper, because I was too embarrassed. It was so silly of me to think that way. If I'd thought about it properly, I would only have received help, support and sympathy.

People from AA phoned me, but I blanked their calls. I used to see their numbers flashing up on my screen and I ignored them all. It got to the stage I didn't even answer calls from a 'private number' in case it was someone from my meetings.

Mentally, I was in a 'bad place' for a few months, and I had to sort it out. Football gave me a release, but there was disappointment from that as well when Morton lost to Peterhead in the promotion play-offs. That defeat was a sore one, as I felt it was my fault, being one of the most experienced players in the team. I was failing in life and failing in football. It played a part in my suicide bid on the M8. Between the football, arguing with Claire and IT, I decided suicide was my best option. But I couldn't even get that right – couldn't turn the steering wheel.

However, I was not for running away any more. I had to challenge my problems, and the suicide moment was a major turning point in my life. I had arrested my problems with drink and drugs, and now I had to sort out IT. Going back to AA was the first step. It wasn't going to cure anything, though. As one guy in AA told me very early on, 'AA can help you to stop drinking, but it can't fix your telly.' However, going back to meetings was a step in the right direction.

When I went to an AA meeting for the first time after my spell away, I met wee Lizzie, a gem of a woman. She had been there for me so many times in the past, and I burst out crying when I met her in the back room. We had a wee blether, and then I went into the main room. I had that mad look in my eyes, but getting my fears and problems out into the open made me feel so much better. I got out of bed the next day feeling much more positive. Quite simply, I wanted to live again, because I felt I had support and people wanted to see me pull through that dark and depressing period.

A series of events then led me to psychologist Angela Maguire. A woman I confided in called Denise put me in touch with her. GPs don't have the time to deal with every patient – I'm told that they only have an average of five or six minutes per patient. I needed more attention than that. I'd been to see a few doctors, but for a variety of reasons it just didn't work out. Most prescribed antidepressants – that was their way of dealing with my problems. So, I phoned Angela. It was my last throw of the dice. I'd had so many disappointments in my attempts to tackle IT that I don't think I would have had it in me to suffer another defeat. I didn't know what to do and needed help. Thankfully, getting in touch with Angela was one of the best things I ever did. She gave me the confidence to confront and blow IT away.

2

MY CHILDHOOD TORMENT

MY CHILDHOOD trauma happened when I was six or seven years old. I can't remember for sure.

IT was abuse of a sexual nature. It happened on two, possibly three, occasions. The guy who abused me used to hang about the streets of Castlemilk and was often there when I was playing with my friends. Where I grew up, kids of all different ages would be out in the street – the boys playing football or hide and seek and the girls skipping or playing hopscotch. There was a real sense of freedom and trust in the area, and the danger from traffic was our parents' main worry. Back in the 1970s, the issue of child abuse was hardly referred to and was regarded as something of a taboo. There was no concern about sexual abuse, not like there is now, when society makes us fearful about what kind of people are living in our neighbourhoods or coming into contact with our children.

I have no idea how I ended up alone with this guy. When he abused me, it was always up a close, nearby to where I'd been playing. At that time, I had no true concept of what age an adult was. I might reckon a person was 25 and they were actually 45, or vice versa. From memory, I thought this guy was between 18 and 22. He was a well-known face to the kids and no doubt to the adults, too. He lived in Castlemilk and obviously had built up trust with the youngsters in the area. He was not a relative or a family friend. He was just a guy I knew from being around the streets.

On the occasions he took me up the close, he would touch me in my groin area and take hold of my hands to touch him. I knew it wasn't right, knew it shouldn't be happening to me, but I was scared. Terrified, to be more exact. I knew I couldn't let it happen any longer, and I used to avoid being near the guy or coming into contact with him in any way. What I couldn't escape, what never left me, was the horrible, sickening smell up the close that he used to take me to. I can't remember what the stench was, but it was awful.

When you're the age I was back then, you don't know what's happening to you. You're just frightened and confused. I used to blame myself and would think that it was my fault it had happened. I used to wonder if I had encouraged the monster to do this to me. All sorts of different emotions and thoughts went through my head.

Amidst the confusion, one thing I was sure about was that I couldn't let anyone know what had happened. There was no way I could tell my dad because the first thing he would have done would have been to hunt the guy down and rip him apart, limb from limb. I have no doubts whatsoever, my dad would have killed him. I didn't want to cause trouble. I was all mixed up. I didn't want a murder on my conscience – to see my dad go to jail for something that I blamed myself for. I didn't want to be the cause of my mum being without her husband and the rest of our family being deprived of their dad. I didn't want any more lives ruined. So, I kept the abuse to myself and hoped it would go away. It never did.

For more than 25 years, it tormented me. The sleepless nights. The guilt. The anger. So many different emotions have haunted me. I continued to blame myself for allowing it to happen. I've beaten myself up over it and let it ruin huge chunks of my life. It has also had a knock-on effect on my footballing career.

The chances are I would have turned out to be an alcoholic anyway. However, I believe the abuse I suffered contributed to me turning to drink for comfort and to blank out the horrible memories. I could also never bring myself to watch a television programme on the subject of child abuse. I would immediately switch the channel if one came on. And if there was a story about sexual abuse in a newspaper, I'd turn the page.

As I grew up, I also feared that I would develop into an abuser because I was abused as a child. It was a horrid thing to carry around, particularly when I became a father. But I had to live with those awful thoughts day after day after day.

The first person I told about the abuse was Claire. I was up in Dundee when I called her back at the house in Glasgow. I was drunk, of course. Claire was giving me a hard time about my drinking, and I suddenly told her about what had happened to me as a kid. Part of the reason was to get her off my back, but I must also have really wanted to tell her to unburden myself. However, I never finished the conversation, and when I woke up the next day I regretted mentioning it to her because I worried what she would think of me.

Since then, of course, we've chatted about it a few times, and Claire has tried to get me to open up a bit more, but she knows that it is up to me to mention it when I feel comfortable. It has to be on my terms.

As I got older and there was no sign that it would disappear from my mind, I knew I had to sort it out. I visited different doctors and was prescribed antidepressants and Valium at different stages. But that wasn't getting to the root of the problem. Again, it was only postponing things. And then the Big Man upstairs put Angela Maguire[1], a wonderful, considerate, warm and intelligent lady, in my path.

My first meeting with Angela was at my house. She came into the living room, and I offered her a handshake. She said, 'I don't do handshakes,' and promptly gave me a hug. I liked that.

Right away, I felt relaxed and totally comfortable in her presence. Most importantly, I was able to open up and tell her absolutely everything. Within two minutes of chatting to her, I knew things were going to work out in my favour. The other thing I liked was that Angela listened when I spoke and would then make points and ask relevant questions, which made me search deep inside myself for the answers I needed to find. In the past, I got the impression that some doctors sat with a clipboard and nodded at me patronisingly. This was different.

Not long into our meeting, she nailed me and pinpointed that I suffered from low self-esteem and was a 'people pleaser', agreeing to do things I didn't really want to do. She said, 'Andy, all of it stops today.' Angela then took a call on her mobile phone, which gave me the chance to go and make a cup of tea. As I waited for the kettle to boil, I was so happy and thought, 'Yes, she's the one. Yes, it does *all* stop today.'

My session with Angela was only supposed to last for an hour, but it went on for 90 minutes longer. At the end of our meeting, I offered her money to cover the cost of two and a half hours. She started to laugh and accused me of people pleasing again. She assured me that it was not about clock watching, it was about getting my head straight and conquering my problems.

When she left my place, I was absolutely floating. Along with the birth of my sons, it was the best buzz I'd ever had. I phoned a couple of my good friends from AA to tell them that I had made a significant breakthrough, and they were delighted. But they also warned me not to get too high, as it made the comedown more difficult to tackle.

After a few more sessions with Angela, things continued to improve. I was able to establish that what I had recalled happening up the close was *all* that happened to me. Before confirming that, I had been unsure if anything further had taken place. Had it gone beyond the 'touching' and ended up much more physical? That was a question I often asked myself, but after opening up to Angela she knew that there was no more to it.

Angela Maguire: Throughout my working career, I have found the incidence of sexual assault or abuse to be much greater than is perceived by the general public. These incidents can range from inappropriate touching to full-blown intentional assault. The trauma felt by the victim will be to some extent influenced by their own levels of sensitivity.

Child victims of abuse often suffer a range of emotional imbalances. They feel different, alone, unable to share all of themselves and experience guilt at not having tried to stop things sooner, not having told someone, as well as feelings of shame, self-rejection, denial and a sense of disempowerment. Their adult self forgets that as a child they perhaps trusted more, were frightened of the consequences, were too ashamed to tell anyone, not being sure of the response that would be given, and were traumatised by what was going on. Many abuse victims, through a sense of hopelessness, turn to substances to mask their pain and turmoil. The first step is always to face the truth.

Andy has been prepared to be true to himself and to work on catching up with some of the joy in his life in spite of the challenges. With the support of his partner Claire and his children, he has much to look forward to.

I have had the privilege of witnessing transformation in the lives of many who have been victims and believe that within every challenge lies opportunity for change and transformation.

Opening up to Angela was great, but I did end up in a bit of a comfort zone and stopped doing the basics an alcoholic has to do every day. I wasn't attending AA meetings and refused to push myself. Basically, I became lazy. It took a lot of effort from me to get back into my good habits, and I'm in a good place just now. I can't believe a lad from Castlemilk is using a phrase such as 'in a good place'. That just doesn't seem right.

Don't get me wrong, I still have bad moments concerning what happened in my childhood. But I know how to 'manage' it. Angela told me I had to stop letting the man control my life, and that I had to reverse the roles and take the power away from him. I'm now able to do this, whereas before meeting Angela I was letting him control things.

I know that I've forgiven myself for laying the blame at my own doorstep for what happened. And I've had to sort of forgive him to be able to move on. But for all I know, he could still be doing it and making some other poor kid's life a misery. I don't even know if I am his only victim or if there's been another hundred in my shoes.

You know, there was a time less than ten years ago that it got on top of me so much that I thought about getting a gun and shooting the guy if I could find him. I don't want to go back into that territory. I know the guy's name, but I don't want this to become a witch-hunt. I don't even know if he's dead or alive. The guy has it on his conscience, and it's up to him how he deals with it.

In many ways, I also count myself to be fortunate that nothing more extreme happened to me. Some children have lost their lives at the hands of sexual predators. Parents have been robbed of their kids because of these sick individuals. What I do want to get out of telling this part about my life is that if any person has been the victim of abuse and is struggling to deal with it, please speak to someone. It might not seem like it, but there are people out there able to help. You needn't be scared that the police will become involved if you don't want them to. Perhaps start by telling your doctor and then take it from there.

It took a lot of soul-searching for me to speak out about this. I'm a footballer and supposed to be a macho man. Only glamorous things happen to guys in my profession, right? Wrong.

It's not been easy for me to open up in public, and I was apprehensive about how my children would react to this subject. It's such a sensitive and personal area to go into, but I felt it was best not to sweep it under the carpet. If me speaking out about this and bringing it to light encourages one person to get over the trauma of being abused, then I'll be a happy man. I feel as though I would have been neglecting my duty if I failed to write about this.

Perhaps some people will feel that I should go all the way and report his name to the police. I know that there is pressure on the government to introduce a law that informs people if paedophiles are living in their area. I can fully understand why parents would want this information. But at this moment in time, I'm not ready to move to that next stage. It's taken me twenty-five years to speak out about the abuse I suffered, and it has to be one step at a time. I need to take into account the feelings of my family just now. They have to come first, and this is the way we have decided to deal with it. I hope people respect my reasoning on this and understand where I'm coming from.

Another reason I decided that it was the right thing to do is because of something that happened a few years back. I'll never forget when a man in his early 30s approached me in Glasgow city centre one afternoon not long after I admitted to being an alcoholic and was receiving professional help to get me through it and then help me to cope with it permanently. The guy said, 'Andy, I read your story in the paper about how you are going to try to stop drinking and lead a better life for you and your family, and from that day on you have inspired me to do the same. I'm now receiving treatment to stop drinking, and I feel great. I'm a Celtic supporter, but you are my hero.' He shook my hand and was gone.

I felt great after that. To be told by another adult that I had inspired him to try to improve his quality of life was an unbelievable feeling. I was floating and on such an incredible high.

I'm not looking to be stopped in the street and congratulated for speaking about abuse, but I hope it can lead to some good for others who have been through the same pain as me and are still experiencing it. Believe me, it's never too late to help yourself. Don't let these abusers ruin your life for a moment longer. And never forget that what happened to you was not your fault. Remember, you are the victim, not the offender. What happened to me when I was just six or seven was not my fault. I only wish I had been able to tell myself that a lot sooner. It would have saved me and my family a lot of heartache.

Note

1. Angela Maguire MA has worked as a psychologist and stress-management consultant for more than 20 years. She has worked with the full range of human problems, including addictive behaviour. She employs a spiritually based holistic approach, and her clients benefit from her unique laser-like intuition for identifying the root cause, before she addresses the secondary problems, which are often the presenting problem. Her passion is to enable her clients to find true balance, harmony and independence in their lives. She works in both the public and private sectors, running self-development courses and seminars, and also works with individual clients.

3

GROWING UP IN CASTLEMILK

I WAS born on 5 June 1973 at Belvedere Hospital in Glasgow's east end. I suppose it is ironic that Belvedere was a mental hospital, but they also had a maternity unit at that time. My parents were just 17 when I was born, and they lived with my mum's folks in Parkhead until they found a place of their own. So, my first known address was 1234 London Road, a free-kick away from Celtic Park.

My parents weren't flush with cash and were on the breadline at that time, so I spent the first few weeks of my life sleeping in a drawer. I remember my parents telling me this when I was about seven, and I had visions of them putting me in beside the underwear and closing the drawer! Of course, it wasn't like that. They made it into a little bed for me, and they assured me I was comfortable and slept well in my little cubby hole.

A few months later, my parents got a house of their own, and we moved to a council house at 2 Ardencraig Road in Castlemilk in the south side of Glasgow. Castlemilk has a reputation as one of the most deprived areas in Scotland and occasionally receives a mention when surveys are printed for the most rundown areas in Britain and even beyond. There's no denying that it is rough and ready, but like many of Glasgow's socially deprived areas – Maryhill, Drumchapel, Easterhouse – I believe it also has a real warmth about it.

When I was growing up, we stayed in a close where the neighbours kept an eye out for one other and would help each other out with a cup of sugar or a pint of milk if someone was short. It was a great area for making friends, and every boy in the street just wanted to play football. From the age of two, I had a ball at my feet. I didn't need anything else – didn't want anything else. We'd play out on the street, or we would have a kick-around in the back gardens. We'd use the washing-line poles for goals, and we'd spend hours playing. We'd sometimes raid the bins for old newspapers and spend ages ripping them up into thousands of little pieces. We'd then climb to the top floor of the close overlooking the back garden, throw the paper over the edge and shout 'Argentina'. We'd do that as our way of making it a big-game atmosphere when we were playing a wee tournament between ourselves. It was our way of marking the final.

The 1978 World Cup finals is my earliest memory of watching football on television, and I was impressed by the way the fans used to throw ticker-tape in the air, some of it settling on the grass while the game was going on. We loved copying them, but it really used to annoy the neighbours, as they hated the mess we left.

As I grew older, I progressed to playing on football pitches and used to love Sunday afternoons. A few of us would head out for a game, which would start as five-a-side. Within half an hour, there could be as many as twenty players in each team, with an age range of anything between five and fifty years old. The pitch would be jam-packed – like a scene from that daft Carling advert – and there'd be bodies everywhere. You were lucky to get a touch of the ball, and when you did you only had time to boot it and move it on. None of this bringing it down, taking a touch and looking up to pick a pass.

As the play raged on at one end, you'd often find a wee group huddled together at the other, having a blether about what they were doing the night before or what their plans were for the coming week. To be honest, for some people it was more of a social gathering. And there would always be a couple of bottles of Irn-Bru doing the rounds with everyone jostling to get a mouthful. Then, the highlight of the day was getting home to watch *Scotsport*. Because there wasn't the same amount of football on television back then that there is now, every programme seemed like a special occasion and was something all football fans looked forward to watching. I loved *Sportscene* on a Saturday night with Archie MacPherson and *Scotsport* the next day with Arthur Montford and Ian Archer.

The perfect scenario on a Sunday was if your mum had the dinner ready just as *Scotsport* was starting. It meant you only had one hour away from playing your game and could get back out again as soon as the trumpet blew to signal the beginning of the theme tune. It was all about doing everything possible to make sure you had as much time playing football as you could manage. Most of the time I'd gulp my dinner down to get back out or I'd put the final few bits and pieces of food into some slices of bread to make a sandwich and run out the door eating it on my way back to the pitch.

I was playing for the school team by the time I was six. I also used to go and watch Clyde on a Saturday afternoon at Shawfield. My dad was friendly with Derek Atkins, the Clyde goalie at the time, and me and my younger brother Johnny would go along to the matches with him. Their manager at that time was Craig Brown, and they had a smashing team. Pat Nevin and Robert Reilly played for them, and they always entertained. I can remember they once played in front of a crowd of 10,000 in a derby match against Partick Thistle. Mo Johnston played for the Jags that day.

My dad was a Rangers fan, and my mum came from a Celtic family. My mum must have won the battle, though, because we were sent to a Catholic school, St Dominic's Primary School in Castlemilk. Despite the fact I became a Celtic fan, my first football strip was a Rangers one, and my dad was keen for me to support his side. My earliest memory of being at a game with him was when he took me to see Rangers against Hibs in a Scottish Cup final replay in 1979. Rangers won 3–2, and I started to cry with fear when my dad threw me up in the air every time they scored.

He also took me to their old training ground at the Albion, in the shadows of Ibrox Stadium. The fearsome Jock Wallace was the manager at the time, and I remember watching John Greig and Bobby Russell train that day. We stayed behind to get autographs from Davie Cooper and Jim Bett – otherwise known as Jazzer – as they came off the pitch. Coops and Bett were my dad's favourite players, and I'm proud to say I ended up playing with Bett at Dundee United. What a great guy Jazzer was. When I used to watch him, he always struck me as being dour-faced, but when I got to know him I discovered that Jim's sense of humour was wicked. A great guy.

My dad was a massive Gers fan, but try as hard as he could he just couldn't get me to follow in his footsteps. Celtic became my team. Both my grans stayed close to Parkhead, and when I went to visit them I'd sneak in to watch Celtic play.

My favourite memory as a Celtic fan was the day they won the league on the final day of the 1985–86 season. Hearts lost 2–0 to Dundee at Dens Park, and Celtic thumped St Mirren 5–0 at Love Street. That was a dramatic day, and I was one of the Celtic fans who invaded the pitch to celebrate at full time. In fact, I was caught running onto the pitch by STV's footage of the game. I couldn't believe it as I watched myself in action on the telly the next day. It was my TV debut, and I was starring on *Scotsport*!

It was my dream to earn a living on the pitch, and from about the age of ten I felt it was going to be a reality. I was a good pupil – well, at primary school at least – and I gave it my best shot. I was never any trouble to the teachers and was able to do all my work. But being more than half-decent at football earned you crucial street cred in Castlemilk, and that seemed just as important as credit from the teachers. It was a real no-no to be considered brainy, and anyone who showed any level of educational aptitude would end up more often than not being bullied. Terrible but true. So, if you couldn't play football, you had to be able to fight. Few were able to do both.

Because I was a decent footballer, the only scraps I became involved in were with my brother Johnny. I also have a younger sister, Denise, and another brother, Jamie. The four of us used to share a bedroom. There were two sets of bunk beds, a black-and-white telly with an Atari, a snooker table and our dog Sheba all in one tiny room. It was too congested, and poor old Sheba got the heave-ho after less than six months. The snooker table was about four foot long and stood in the middle of the room. How we managed to play a decent game, God only knows. Usually, the window had to be open to let the cue hang out while you played a shot or else it would be halfway up the wall, as there was no room when the ball was tight to the cushion.

Four kids in a tiny bedroom inevitably caused friction. Johnny and I would often let rip and have a square-go. I remember when I was eight I threw a tin of salmon at him, and it caught him flush on the head. He was a couple of years younger than me and screamed the place down as I held my hand over his mouth and told him not to tell our mum. Another time, Johnny threw a padlock at me, and as I ducked it flew through our bedroom window. That was the final straw for my folks. We needed to get out and move to a bigger house.

Eventually, when I was 11, we relocated to 12 Ardencraig Road to a three-bedroom place – or should that be palace? It was just what we needed, and I was especially pleased for Denise. She needed her own space, away from her crazy brothers.

The bedlam and overcrowding in our first home was nothing compared to what it was like when we used to go on family holidays to Saltcoats, down the Ayrshire coast. Honestly, we'd go there for a week, and there would be fifteen of us crammed into a one-bedroom flat: aunties, uncles, cousins, grannies, the lot. Some nights, ten of us would sleep in the same bed. And that was our idea of getting away from the hustle and bustle of the city!

It's different now in terms of holidays. The whole world is out there, and it's easy to travel to exotic destinations with cheap flights and package deals. Back then, we were delighted with a break down the Ayrshire coast. We would have fun on the beach and paddle in the Irish Sea.

I'd be given 50p spending money every day, and once it was gone, it was gone. It was a good way of making me realise the value of money and how to make it last. I'd usually buy an ice cream and go for a round of putting.

At the September weekend break, we'd head down to Blackpool on the coach from Buchanan Street bus station. What a laugh that was. Just about everybody got blitzed on the bus, and there'd be card schools and all sorts going on. I remember one couple fell out on the journey because the guy lost the weekend's spending money at poker.

My parents worked hard to give us what they could, and I'll always be grateful to them for that. Dad worked in Beattie's Bakery, and then he became a scaffolder. I used to love Friday afternoons, as we would jump on the number 46 bus from Castlemilk to Duke Street to his work, where we'd always be given a bag of cakes. Sometimes, I'd go from there and stay at my granny Betty's house. She was great. She'd spoil me rotten with sweets, chocolate biscuits, Coco Pops and juice, and let me stay up late to watch the late-night horror movie. Sadly, she died suddenly when she was just 55 after failing to recover from a heart attack. I was 12 at the time, and it cut me up. I was close to her, and her death was the first time I felt a real sense of loss in my life. My dad took it badly. Losing his mum at that age couldn't have been easy for him.

Mum stayed at home to look after the kids. She's had quite a life of it, having me so young and then two more children by the time she was twenty-two. But I never once heard her complain. She was always there for us, and is a loving and caring woman.

Our clothes would be washed and ironed and our dinner was always on the table. She was fantastic on the sewing machine and would often make curtains and different things for relatives and neighbours to give her an extra bit of pocket money.

There's no doubt that she worried about us all, as Castlemilk could be an unforgiving place. There would often be gang fights and other unsavoury incidents. One of the first attacks I can remember was a policeman getting a bottle of Irn-Bru smashed over his head after some guy tried to resist arrest. The gang fights were also a bit tasty. The 'Bundy' and the 'Craig' would battle to protect their honour and their patch. They'd meet at the top of the hill in the local park and get wired in. Usually, a couple of bottles of Buckfast and a few cans of lager would be drunk to get them going – the swords and bricks would come later. No prisoners were taken, and you had to be brave or stupid to get involved. That kind of thing was a way of life for a few guys, and the same ones would be in and out of jail for the gang fights and fighting with the police. As usual, a few kiddy-on merchants would turn up, pretending to want to get involved, but they were quickly sussed out by the real players and put firmly in their place.

Despite the violence and mayhem, there was respect shown between neighbours, and there was an unspoken element of trust between people. We used to leave a key hanging on a piece of string behind the letterbox so me and my brothers and sister could all come and go as we pleased. There was never a thought that somebody could use the key to burgle our house. For all the trouble and unsavoury incidents, there was a line drawn that people knew not to cross.

After living in a few different places because of my job, I'm now back in Castlemilk and have settled there. At this stage of my life, I don't feel the need to be anywhere else, as there's something about Castlemilk I can't seem to let go of. I was born and raised there, and despite some of the drawbacks that come with living in a deprived area, I still regard it as my true home.

4

THE WORLD AT MY FEET

FOOTBALL HAS been in my blood since the day I was born. My dad was a terrific player and was offered the chance to sign for Ipswich Town straight from school after going on trial at Portman Road. Sir Bobby Robson was the manager at that time, but my dad – a talented midfielder – turned down their offer as he felt homesick after just a few days down south.

When I was old enough to understand, he told me about the chance he passed up in England, and I took Ipswich on as my adopted English team. They had a great side in the late 1970s and early '80s, with players such as Arnold Mühren, Frans Thijssen, John Wark, Mick Mills and Paul Mariner.

But my favourite player when I was growing up was Kenny Dalglish. He had the lot: he was brave; he had vision and a world-class ability to turn his marker inside out; he was lethal in front of goal; and he was a brilliant strike partner to the likes of Ian Rush.

My first introduction to an organised game was with St Dominic's when I was in primary three. The manager put me on at left-half, and I was so excited. Unfortunately, I never got to touch the ball, as the ref blew for full time within 60 seconds of me coming on. Still, my career as a footballer was underway, and though my debut lasted less than a minute my roller coaster career was off and running. It progressed from there, and later that year I scored with a header as we beat our fiercest rivals Castleton 6–5.

I also received my first red card for battling with someone in my own team! When I was about ten, I started lashing out at my brother Johnny on the pitch after we got into a row. Johnny was a goalkeeper and had talent between the sticks. I was banned for two games for that incident after being sent to a disciplinary hearing, where I was quizzed by a panel of five teachers. How ridiculous was that?

I joined Clyde Boys Club by the time I was seven and played for them regularly. And my love for the game reached new heights at primary school when Jim and Andy took charge. They bought nets and corner flags for our home games – it was a dream at that age to score into a net. It felt like we were playing at Wembley.

I always struggled to get to sleep on a Friday night before a game. I'd be up polishing my boots and making sure they were absolutely gleaming. I took my football seriously and wanted to look the part as well as catch the eye with good performances. The proudest moment of my early career was when we won the Glasgow Cup after beating Our Lady of Lourdes 2–1 in the final at Roseberry Park. I played at sweeper and was the organiser on the pitch!

Football wasn't my only sport. I enjoyed tennis and golf during the summer holidays. When Wimbledon was on, we'd all be out on the street pretending to be John McEnroe, Björn Borg or Jimmy Connors. My golfing career was restricted to skipping on at Linn Park with a few of my mates – we'd have about four clubs between six of us.

When I was 11, Clyde sent me for trials with the Strathclyde League Select, and I made it into the team to play against sides from Dundee, Aberdeen and Ayrshire. It was a good opportunity to put myself in the shop window, and I was approached by Celtic to join their boys club.

Eastercraigs Boys Club, a well respected and successful team in the Glasgow area, also asked me to join, and I was flattered, but I stayed with Clyde. I was comfortable with them at that time, felt a bit of loyalty and didn't want to abandon them after the first offer came in. However, I did leave Clyde when I was approaching 13 to join Rangers Amateurs. We trained at Ibrox, and my dad was delighted to see me wearing his favourite jersey.

Rangers offered me the chance to sign an S Form in the summer of 1986. They took me in, gave me a tour of the trophy room and did everything to persuade me that Ibrox was the best place to further my career. Graeme Souness and Walter Smith had just taken over, and it was the start of the Gers revolution. They did ask me about my religion, but being Catholic wasn't a problem to them. Rangers said they were moving on from that policy. John Spencer was already on their books, and the fact he was a Catholic was getting him a lot of attention at that time.

Naturally, my dad wanted me to sign, and he was proud that I was being given the chance to forge a career there. But I decided that it wasn't the right move to join Rangers at that stage of my life. I was never quite comfortable with the idea of being at a Catholic secondary school – St Margaret Mary's – and being a Rangers player.

A few years later, though, I regretted my decision. Guys such as Neil Murray, Craig Flannigan and David Hagen were in my age group at youth level, and they all signed for Rangers. It worked out well for them, because before they were twenty the three-foreigner rule was introduced to European football, and it meant opportunities had to be given to Scottish players. They made a right few quid from one-off games – in the region of £20,000 for qualifying for the Champions League, for example. That kind of dosh would have been welcome at such a young age. I reckon I would have gone on and played for the first team, as I believe I was every bit as talented as those guys.

Hearts also offered me the chance to sign an S Form with them, but they weren't professional in the way they went about their business. They asked me to make my own way through to Tynecastle, chap the front door and ask for Alex MacDonald. Sorry, but I wasn't doing that.

And Hamilton Accies invited me in for signing talks, which was a bizarre experience. I went along to Douglas Park with my dad to meet John Lambie, the Hamilton manager. I'll be honest: being in his company frightened me. I can't quite put my finger on exactly why I felt that way about him, and I'm sure he's a decent bloke. Lambie was raging with his chairman Jan Stepek that night. For some bizarre reason, the Douglas Park director was on the pitch playing golf! He was hitting iron shots from one penalty box to the other, and there was steam coming out of Lambie's ears as he watched from the side of the park. The whole thing was hysterical.

Clyde also showed an interest, and my mum still has the letters from then boss Craig Brown, trying to persuade me to sign. There was an emotional pull there from my younger days, and I was sorely tempted. Manchester United also sniffed about and asked me down for the school holidays, but as I'd already committed myself to another club I couldn't take it any further.

It was quite a time in the McLaren household with so many teams chasing after my signature. Johnny is two years younger than me, and he was also attracting a lot of attention. By then, he had ditched the gloves and was playing outfield as a midfielder and an attacker. Scouts were constantly at our door in Castlemilk, and Mum and Dad must have felt they were running a café, as they constantly had to entertain them with cups of tea and custard creams! We ended up quite famous with the locals. I became known as 'Andy the footballer'. Manchester United also came in for Johnny, and he spent two weeks down there training at the Cliff.

I had also been training for a couple of years with Dundee United, and I felt comfortable there. Graeme Liveston was in charge of the 14–16-year-old players, and he was an excellent coach. I played for Hamilton Thistle, the feeder team used by United to ensure that their players received the kind of football education they wanted them to have. Most of the training sessions were on AstroTurf at Helenvale Park, in the shadow of Celtic Park. United had a reputation for giving youth a chance, and that's why I opted to sign for them when I was 13.

Not long after signing, I went up to Dundee during the school holidays and quickly discovered that I didn't fancy being away from home. I wanted out and immediately regretted my decision to choose United. I told Mum and Dad, and we looked into the possibility of cancelling my contract. Easier said than done. I had hardly reached puberty, but I think even at schoolboy age wee Jim McLean had tied me down on a ten-year deal! So, I had no choice but to get on with it.

At 14, I was already being told by the United staff that I was going to cut it as a professional. My game was in good shape, and I was keen to listen and learn. I was enjoying my football, but around that time I was also, sadly, starting to enjoy a drink. I began boozing when I was 12 – a couple of cans of Tennents or Carlsberg here and there. Two years on and that had progressed into a steady routine of drinking at the weekend and during the week, and it was already more than just two cans per session. I was playing football constantly and also selling the *Daily Record* and *Sunday Mail* at night as the punters came out of the pub. I made good money doing that. But I was tired, what with school, football and drinking. It must have shown, as Liveston asked me to give up my paper job. I told him I would, but it was my only source of income, and I couldn't afford to.

What I did effectively give up at that stage was my education. I hardly attended school and would spend the mornings and afternoons with my mates. The remainder of my education was the first of many things alcohol took from me.

I suppose the teachers who worried about what could have happened to me must have breathed a sigh of relief during the summer of 1989 when Scotland hosted the Under-16 World Cup finals. The Scotland squad, under the leadership of Craig Brown and Ross Mathie, became household names. We were on the front and back pages of the national newspapers and headline news on the telly. It was pretty weird but exciting all the same.

We made it to the final against Saudi Arabia and played in front of more than 50,000 at Hampden Park, not to mention the hundreds of thousands who watched on TV. But the tournament got off to quite a slow start, and it took a while for us to gather momentum. Our first game was against Ghana, and we played out a dull 0–0 draw in front of about 8,000 spectators. The highlight of the day was meeting Pelé during the formalities on the pitch before kick-off. It was an honour for a teenage kid from Castlemilk to meet the great man, and he came across as a really genuine guy. Players from that generation all tend to be gentlemen. I remember, for example, meeting Jim Baxter at a Scottish Football Writers' Association dinner, and he came up to me and Robbie Winters and shook our hands. He said that he knew who we were, and I just about melted. I told Slim he was a hero of my dad's, and he seemed chuffed. I also met Jimmy Johnstone a couple of times, and the wee man was a pleasure to be around. Jinky had time for everyone and made them all feel special. Baxter and Johnstone were genuine Scottish football legends, and they're both sorely missed.

We were nervous during that game against Ghana, which was to be expected, I suppose. I played wide on the right, but I didn't really perform well that day. I was pleased to be back in that position, though. In a tournament we played in the build-up to the World Cup, we faced Italy, and I was asked to perform a man-marking job on their playmaker. It felt strange being a hatchet man for 90 minutes! But Craig Brown praised me for my performance – my opponent didn't get a sniff.

Our next game was at Fir Park against Cuba, and we beat them 3–0. We were off and running and never looked back. Our last group game was again in Motherwell, and we drew 1–1 with Bahrain, which was enough to take us through to the next stage as Group A runners-up.

The interest from the whole country was growing by the day. It was phenomenal, to be honest, and we all felt really proud to be part of it. We were being asked to do all sorts of stuff for the newspapers. They seemed to be interested in getting every last drop out of us. For example, we had to fill in a questionnaire about our likes and dislikes, hobbies, etc. When asked about my taste in music, I wanted to say Pink Floyd, but I thought I'd be slaughtered for it, so I copied a couple of the other boys and put in Deacon Blue, even though I couldn't have told you what any of their songs were.

In the quarter-final, we faced East Germany at Pittodrie. We won that tie thanks to a goal from John Lindsay. By the time we came up against Portugal in the semi-final at Tynecastle, it was silly stuff. The kick-off was delayed to let the crowd in. More than 28,000 packed into the stadium that evening. It was absolute bedlam.

Unfortunately, I missed the match through injury. Portugal had Rui Costa and Luís Figo in their side, and they also had a player by the name of Gil, who was their superstar, tipped to be the best of the lot by a long way. It never worked out for him. It just goes to show that it's not only in Scotland that teenagers with enormous potential sometimes don't make what they should out of their career.

It was boiling that night in Edinburgh, and the pitch was bathed in sunshine. The game was live on telly, the media coverage again reaching unbelievable levels. After being piped onto the pitch, we won thanks to a brilliant header from Brian O'Neil. It was an unbelievable feeling – one of my happiest nights in football, without a doubt.

In the final, we were up against Saudi Arabia. I started on the bench, but did get on later. I was so pleased for Brown and Mathie that we had made it so far. Both had put an incredible amount of work into the entire campaign, not just from when the tournament kicked off, but for months and months prior to that. Our preparation was excellent – there was real attention to detail. I also started to learn about good eating habits from being in the national set-up. Before that, I had survived on chips, eggs and sausages, but now I was eating chicken and pasta and plenty of fruit.

I still meet people to this day who say they were at *that* final at Hampden. There were more than 50,000 inside the ground that night. We went two goals up, and it looked like we were going to do it. But they fought back. Brian O'Neil missed a penalty, and before we knew it they'd levelled it. We had little else to give – the emotional and physical strain of the previous two weeks caught up with us for that final half-hour of the game. After extra-time, the final went to a penalty shoot-out, and I was desperate to take one. I looked up to my dad in the stand and held up three fingers to signal I was hitting the third spot-kick. Dad gave me the thumbs up. He looked so proud of me. Mum was nervous and put her head in her hands.

I scored, but we lost. O'Neil missed another penalty in the shoot-out. After the game, a reporter in the press conference asked him, 'How does it feel to have missed a penalty that cost your country the World Cup?' It was bang out of order to ask a young kid a question like that but a lesson to all of us who went on to have a career in the game that the media can make life difficult for you.

So, there were tears of disappointment at the end, but we were immensely proud. I had scored a goal in a World Cup final. It is my claim to fame and can never be taken away from me.

After the final, stories surfaced that the Saudis had at least four players over the age of eighteen in their line-up, but I never believed that for a minute. We lost. Deal with it and move on.

The real tragedy was that more than a few of the lads in the Scotland squad were out of the game by the time they were 19.

It was always going to be a lot to ask that the whole squad make a full-time living from football, but it wasn't acceptable to see so many of the boys fall away so soon. The big question is, of course, who's most to blame – the players or the clubs they signed for?

But I'll never forget the laughs we had. I made good friends, including Billy Dolan and Kevin McGoldrick – top guys who would never see you stuck. I'm also proud of the fact that I was one of only three from the squad who went on to play for the full side. Brian O'Neil and Paul Dickov were the others.

After the final, Gary Bollan and I decided that the best way to get over our World Cup heartache was to drown our sorrows. There was a party at Eddie Conville's house, and before we went Gary and I decided that we'd get a 'cargo' to take with us. Remember, we were two fresh-faced teenagers who earlier that day had taken part in an Under-16 World Cup final and who all week had been pictured in every newspaper in the country! Gary could hardly believe my cheek as I walked up to the counter and ordered a dozen cans of lager and a bottle of vodka. The woman behind the till took my money, gave me a knowing smile and said, 'I wiz dead proud of you today, son. I thought youz were brilliant.' What a laugh!

I was flying when I arrived for pre-season training at United three weeks later. My debut was against Tayport Juniors in a friendly. I played well and felt great about myself. Paul Sturrock pulled me aside after the game and said that I had a right good chance of going all the way. I think it was the first and last compliment he ever paid me.

The unshakeable belief I had from about the age of ten that I was going to be a footballer was well on its way to becoming a reality. Jim McLean gave me my first deal when I was fifteen – a three-year contract worth £45 a week plus £12 expenses and a signing-on fee of £450. Hardly Beckham at LA Galaxy proportions, but it was a start.

Earning some money was nice, but I quickly got a taste of the other side of life as a footballer at United when we were fined our £10 win bonus after we defeated Brechin 5–0 at Glebe Park in the BP Youth Cup. We were 5–0 up at half-time, but wee Jim wasn't happy. He told us at full-time that we would not be receiving our bonus money, as we had let our standards slip in the second half. I couldn't believe it. Genuinely, I was gobsmacked.

They took the BP Youth Cup seriously at United. I'd go so far as to say that just as much emphasis was put on that tournament as was put on first-team games. Honestly. A lot of careers were ruined at United because of perceived underachievement in the BP Youth Cup. McLean took it as a real marker as to whether or not you could make the grade as a first-team player.

I got off to a great start in the tournament when, just an hour after agreeing my first contract in an office at Love Street, McLean told me to go down to the changing-rooms and get ready, as I was playing that night in the semi-final against St Mirren. Hardly ideal preparation, but we won 3–1, and I scored the first goal. Vinnie Arkins got the other two.

We played Celtic in the final at Tannadice, and we battered them. I played the 90 minutes but sadly missed a few sitters. We lost 1–0. Stevie Fulton played for Celtic that night, only a few days after he'd played in the Scottish Cup semi-final against Hibs at Hampden, and helped Billy McNeill's side win 3–0. Thankfully, we went on to win two cups in a row and the reserve-league title as well. We were a talented bunch of players and credit must go to the United set-up for bringing so many players through the system and giving them an opportunity in the first team.

5

EARLY YEARS AT TANNADICE

MY NINE-YEAR association with Dundee United started in June 1989 when I left Glasgow to join the Tannadice club full time. I had just turned 16 and was nervous about leaving home, which I suppose is natural when any young kid moves away from their parents. But the apprehension was mixed with excitement. For as long as I could remember, I wanted to become a professional footballer, and my dream became a reality that summer.

I left home on the Sunday afternoon with a small sports bag packed with some clothes to do me for the week until I came back down the road the following Friday night. I kissed and hugged my parents and my siblings goodbye as I embarked on my first step as my own man in the big – and as I found out – bad world.

A lad called Campbell Clark was also joining United at around the same time. He was from Ayrshire, and we arranged to meet at Glasgow's Queen Street Station to travel north by train. Campbell was switched on and quite mature for his age, and he dealt with all the arrangements. When we arrived on Tayside, there was no one from United at the train station to meet us and take us to our digs. Thankfully, Campbell had the address, and we took a taxi to our new 'home'.

Tam McMillan was the third player in the digs, and there were two bedrooms to share between us. One of the rooms had bunk-beds, and we used that as our base. Strangely, no one wanted to sleep in the other room alone, so we would take turns sleeping on the floor. We usually sat up chatting, talking about the training we'd had and what we were going to go through the next day.

It was about a ten-minute walk to Tannadice, and we had to be in for 9 a.m. to get the kit ready for the first-team squad and management. I was probably one of the worst workers on the YTS ground staff. My job was to sweep the home dressing-room floor and pack the kit for the first-team match at the weekend. Of course, I couldn't help myself and tried to cut corners whenever I could. I had a bad habit of packing towels that hadn't been washed into the team hamper.

Paul Sturrock was our immediate gaffer. He was in charge of the reserves and also took a great deal of interest in supervising the guys who had just arrived at the club. Once our ground-staff duties were over for the day, Sturrock would take us out for some extra coaching in the afternoons. I used to reckon it was shite having to go out onto the training pitch and do more training. I wanted to be in the snooker hall or putting a bet on. Sturrock was on my case constantly, and I used to resent the way he pestered us, but in hindsight I can see that I learned so much from the man who was affectionately known as 'Luggy' because of the size of his ears.

We used to do loads of crossing and finishing, and I worked really hard on improving my left foot, the weaker of the two. Sometimes, my cross balls from that side wouldn't even reach the penalty box, but I kept at it, and my left foot eventually became as good as my right. Luggy also taught me different aspects of the game that I hadn't really thought about before, like my movement off the ball, when to go long and when to come short. It was all simple stuff but so effective. He was different class at coaching.

Sturrock obviously took on board plenty of what he'd picked up from Jim McLean. However, on one occasion not long after I'd joined the club, I think the mini-McLean style of management went too far, and it led to me walking out on Dundee United.

After a youth-team game, Sturrock fined me £25 for 'not playing well'. I thought his decision was appalling – it was almost half my week's wages. Right after the match, I headed to White's Bar, near Tannadice, for a booze with my teammate Graham McCheyne. It was our routine on a Thursday – play the youth-team game then nip into White's as soon as we'd showered. We'd arrive at about quarter to ten and try to down six pints of lager before chucking out time at eleven. We'd usually manage it without too much hassle, but it would more often than not lead to us spewing up on the way home. After Luggy's fine, I told Graham that enough was enough and I was chucking it. The next day, I packed my bag and returned to Castlemilk. The club phoned my mum's house and asked me to go back. I told her they were out of order, but my mum encouraged me to get my head down and not throw away my chance to make it as a professional.

So, I returned on the Monday morning and was immediately pulled in to McLean's office after the warm-up. He looked at me and said, 'Don't you ever do that again. You're fined two weeks' wages.'

I was gutted. I was also skint and couldn't afford to pay the fine. I cried during the following training session. McLean ruled by fear, and it took a lot for even the senior professionals to stand up to him. However, when a young lad at a club is being treated that way, I believe the older players have a duty to offer him some protection. Senior guys should try to reason with the manager, but they were obviously too scared at United to confront McLean. Sadly, no one ever stood up to him. The senior players kept their mouths shut. And it wasn't just incidents concerning me: other players were also treated harshly. That really angers me, and it's why in my latter years as a pro I've never stood silent and watched a lad being unfairly treated. I've always stood up for the player and, at the very least, asked the manager or coach to reassess his options.

Paul Sturrock: Andy was a talented laddie, and we knew he had all the attributes to go on and play for the first team. There's no doubt I was hard on him, but it was only for his own good. If I hadn't believed that he had talent, I wouldn't have wasted my time taking him for extra coaching or disciplining him. I was a striker and could see he had ability, knew he had something to offer.

But he had difficulties on setting his sights on becoming a professional footballer. Like a lot of boys from housing schemes, he wanted to have too much of a life outside the game and probably didn't appreciate the chance he was being given.

But he was a nice lad. Always jovial and funny. His was always the loudest voice in the dressing-room, and he enjoyed having a Jack-the-Lad reputation. But there was never any malice in him.

McLean had my card marked from day one at Tannadice. Before my arrival, he phoned my secondary school in Castlemilk and asked for a copy of my attendance records. Needless to say, I was absent quite a bit. I used to go to a mate's house in the morning and spend time with him and a few others for a laugh and a carry on. Or sometimes I'd just go for a kip. My schoolwork suffered, as I preferred being with my mates to being in class. That was when I was about 14 and 15. But in my first two years at secondary school, I was in the top classes for most subjects. I had potential and found that I actually enjoyed the work. I liked English and Modern Studies in particular. However, in Modern Studies, I sometimes used to take bottles of ginger and packets of crisps in and just sit up the back and get wired in. The teacher would also let me go for a sleep at the back of the room if I told him I was tired.

When I was 14, I started to drink alcohol during the week. I was hanging around with boys older than me, and they had a few quid from their giros to spend on booze. Another reason for my lethargy was my late-night paper round. The pubs and chippies were the best places to flog my 100 copies. After a night on the bevvy and selling my paper, I was never hung-over the next day, just tired. And I was never disruptive in school or a bad kid. I was just bored with lessons and studying. I'd rather be out kicking a ball or drinking a can of lager.

Because of my shocking attendance record, McLean said to me, 'I think we're going to have to keep a close eye on you. You're going to give us problems.' He was absolutely right. I gave him even more problems than he could ever have imagined, I suppose.

After training was finished in the afternoon, we'd be clear at about 3.30 p.m. and would head down to the bookies to place a bet on the horses. Mind you, with earnings of £55 a week – although my digs were paid for – I wasn't exactly flush to shell out money. In fact, I earned more cash selling my papers in Castlemilk. How's that for irony? A trainee professional at a Scottish Premier League club earned more by selling the *Daily Record* than he did from the game. Between wages and tips, I pulled in a minimum of £60 per week selling the *Record*, so I took a wage cut to become a footballer!

Most of the time, I was bored and lonely at Dundee United. None of the young players could drive, so we had to find things to do on our own doorstep. I'm constantly fidgety and not the type who is able to sit down and watch the telly at night or go to the video shop and grab a movie. My short attention span wouldn't even allow me to sit through a two-hour film. I could rarely last half an hour watching *EastEnders* or *Coronation Street*. I was the type of guy who had to be on the go. I needed company or something to do to keep me busy. It's only recently that I've managed to train myself to watch a film from start to finish. God, I've missed out on some great movies and no longer need to deprive Claire of a night at the pictures.

Because the nights were so lonely up in Dundee, I would sometimes cry myself to sleep. If truth be told, I hated it. I couldn't wait for Friday afternoon to come so I could make the 80-mile journey back to Glasgow to see Claire, my mates and my family. It was also a chance for me to get drunk without having to go into training in the morning. I was able to sleep it off.

I used to tell my mum I loved it in Dundee and that everything was fine. But it was the last place in the world I wanted to be. I was always skint, usually because I had been fined for something ridiculous. I remember one Friday lunchtime, Alex Cleland was heading back down to Glasgow, and I decided to hitch a lift from him to save me the £15 train fare. I knew I would be fined for leaving too early, but the fine would only be a tenner, so by my crude method of arithmetic I was still saving a fiver. However, the bastards fined me £30. The most annoying thing was that they used to fine me flippantly, as if I was earning £300 a week. They had no idea about the financial struggle I had trying to live from week to week.

One weekend trip back down to Glasgow changed my life for good. It was late October, perhaps early November, and Claire told me she was pregnant. I didn't know how to react, as it wasn't planned. Claire was still 16, the same age as me, and I should have comforted her and held her, as God only knows what she was going through. She was in a total state of shock, but my way of dealing with it was to pretend the pregnancy didn't exist.

It was like when I opened a bill and owed more money than I expected. I'd not look at the bill again in the hope that it would just disappear. It was the same with the news about the baby. All I wanted to do was go out and get drunk – get sozzled, forget about my problems and hopefully wake up in the morning with everything sorted. And it was the same for most weekends after that. It took me ages to come to terms with the pregnancy. I couldn't even bring myself to tell my parents the news. I wasn't sure how they'd react.

Eventually, my folks found out when Claire's mum broke the news to my dad after bumping into him in the local pub a few weeks later. My old man used it as an excuse to have a celebratory drink and a party. I suppose I can identify with his attitude to life on that score. Any excuse for a bevvy.

It was now all out in the open, but I wasn't interested in talking about it. I should have been more supportive to Claire. I just wanted to blank it. I couldn't fully comprehend what becoming a father was all about. Although, what 16-year-old kid would? That said, we never, ever spoke about Claire having an abortion. A termination was never on our agenda.

I just got on with my football, and it was going pretty well. Within a few months, I was playing for the reserves and helping United do well in the youth cups. But my life as I knew it was turned upside down when my dad suddenly died. I had been on the phone to my mum the night before and knew from her voice that something wasn't quite right. She just said to me, 'Andrew, I'll phone you back.' She never did.

After training the following day, McLean pulled me aside and told me to report to his office an hour later. When I arrived, my two uncles, John and Michael, were there. I knew something serious had happened. John, my mum's brother, told me my dad had passed away. McLean left the room to give us some privacy. I cried. It was 14 March 1990.

For some ridiculous reason, the fact that it was Gold Cup day at Cheltenham and Norton's Coin romped in at 100–1 also sticks in my head. I had put a bet on the race the previous afternoon, but, unfortunately, it wasn't on the 100–1 outsider.

We drove down the road and went to my gran's house first. I tried to be strong for the sake of my mum and younger brothers and sister – John was fourteen, Denise was twelve and Jamie was just six. I can also remember going to visit my dad's body at the Co-op funeral parlour near the Kingston Bridge.

My dad was just 33 when he died. He choked on his own vomit after a massive drinking session. He was a popular guy and far too young to die. I don't know if he was an alcoholic. He certainly liked a good drink, but I'm not sure to what extent.

He was buried in Riddrie, in the east end of Glasgow, and on the morning of his funeral I remember my mum saying to me, 'Andrew, please don't get drunk today.' I felt so sorry for her at that moment. She was about to bury her husband and had three children left to look after but she was more worried that her eldest son would let himself get out of control. She'd not had an easy life and had put up with so much. I often remember seeing my dad drunk, and there would be trouble and arguments because of it. I always said to myself, 'I'll never allow myself to get in a state like that.'

I helped lower my dad's coffin into the ground and said my goodbyes to him. Someone came over to me and said, 'Don't worry, you'll be fine.' To this day, I still don't know who it was, but the words helped comfort me during a difficult moment. From that day on, I was the man of two houses – on £55 a week, although Claire would have disagreed with that, as I rarely contributed to her household, financially or emotionally.

United allowed me a couple of weeks off to help my mum sort things out, and it gave me time to grieve. But on my return to Tannadice, the club showed no compassion towards me. They were really cold and didn't ask how I was feeling after my loss. I wasn't looking for sympathy but a little understanding would have been appreciated.

McLean spoke to me the following month and offered me a new contract. It was a four-year deal with a four-year option. It was £145 per week and included a one-off signing-on fee of £5,000. However, I would now have to pay my own digs.

Back then, I was struggling financially and had the baby on the way. Dangling a £5,000 carrot in front of me was massive. The length of the contract and the weekly wage did not really appeal, and the fact I would have to pay my own digs and income tax meant I was probably only going to be about £35 a week better off. But despite my apprehension, I agreed to sign the contract.

With hindsight, I know that I shouldn't have touched it, but I couldn't resist the money, particularly the lump sum.

Paul Sturrock: We knew Andy had plenty to contend with during his first year at United, and he suffered because of that. The second year was better for him, and he seemed to benefit from his younger brother John signing for the club on the ground staff.

At the time, we had a success rate of about 90 per cent of players coming through the youth system at United going on to play for the first team. Jim McLean was a hard taskmaster, and if players weren't doing well, playing to a certain standard, he wanted to know why. I was the first to get it from him, not the players. So, that's another reason why I was so hard on them.

Andy wasn't the only one who caused us problems. John O'Neil and Duncan Ferguson were also a lot of bother. In fact, I usually found that the three of them were involved in incidents together. They were unbelievable, and it was one helluva battle trying to manage them. Their timekeeping, in particular, was poor.

They were late once too often for Jim's liking, and he told me to get the three of them to paint the gymnasium. I gave them pots of paint and brushes and told them to whitewash the gym. They were raging.

After about an hour, I went to see how they were getting on. I couldn't believe it when I walked in. All they'd done was write 'Jim McLean is a cunt' in huge letters on the walls. I couldn't believe it but started to laugh. I told the gaffer to come and see their work, telling him the lads had made an excellent job of the task. Jim came in, took one look at what they'd written and even he started to laugh. Eventually! Credit to them for having the cheek.

Being on Andy's case worked, because he went on to play for the first team very early and played well. He should have kicked on from there, and I believe he should have played many, many times for Scotland. Off-the-field activities prevented him achieving so much more from the game.

Andy eventually got his Scotland cap. John and Duncan also played for Scotland. Players can say what they like about Dundee United at that time, but they received an excellent grounding to build their careers from.

Claire gave birth to our son Dylan on 25 June 1990, and he weighed 8 lb 7oz. It was one of the most amazing feelings I'd ever experienced. We were both nervous about going into hospital for the birth, but I have to say Claire was fantastic. I wish I could say the same about myself.

After the initial high of witnessing Dylan's first few hours of life, I wasn't for hanging around the hospital to help Claire or be a doting dad. My only thought was to get out of there as quickly as possible and join my mates in Castlemilk, because I knew they had a carry-out, and I was desperate for a few beers.

Those first few moments of Dylan's life were symptomatic of my first few years as a parent. I was playing in the first team for United not long after Dylan was born, and it meant I had a wee bit more money in my pocket from the appearance bonuses. However, rather than put it to good use and give Claire a bit extra or make sure my mum was sorted, I was blowing it on booze. I was drinking more and more and was doing myself harm and causing damage to my mind and body, not to mention my relationship with Claire.

The rave scene had just exploded, and I got heavily into it. When I came down to Glasgow from Dundee on a Saturday night, I'd spend the next 24 hours boozing and taking Ecstasy. It took its toll on me, and I was still fucked by the Tuesday and Wednesday. Because of the drink and drugs, my mood swings were incredible. I'd be on a high for a few days and then on an absolute downer for a couple of days afterwards. The downers made me want to quit Dundee United and move back to Glasgow. The comedown from the high of the drugs was unbelievable, and I was unable to think rationally.

Depending on the mood I was in, I could take two, three or four

Ecstasy tablets in a night. I'd be dancing and in a happy mood. The tabs made me feel like I could fly, and everyone taking Es 'loved' each other. I'd usually go to the Metro nightclub in Saltcoats, or there would sometimes be an illegal rave party in a warehouse somewhere. Most of the ravers sipped on bottles of water when they were on Ecstasy, but that wasn't for me. I mixed the drugs with alcohol. I was drunk before I took any and wanted more beer after I'd popped an E.

I didn't particularly like the raves for a couple of reasons. First, I was a rotten dancer and second I couldn't be bothered with all these mad people faffing about drinking water all night. I preferred the after-rave parties. We would all go back to someone's house and everyone would come down from their Es with a few beers.

The music was really hard-core dance, but, to be honest, I hated that kind of stuff. I liked the Happy Mondays' style of music – the rest of it didn't really appeal. But I was wasted and didn't care what I was listening to.

I got into the rave scene through some pals in Castlemilk. Typical Andy – I didn't want to wimp out of taking Ecstasy in case the lads accused me of becoming a 'Billy Big Time'. So, my age-old problem came to the surface again – rather than refusing to get into drugs so that I could concentrate on my career, I followed them like a little sheep.

I was also gambling heavily and blowing a sizeable portion of my wages at the bookies. When I became an established member of the United first team, the afternoon training sessions weren't as frequent, which was great for me, because it meant I had time on my hands to spend in the pub and the bookies. I usually bet on the dogs and the horses. On a few occasions, I'd end up going down the road with no wages left after wasting every penny on drink and betting. I was earning about £300 per week at United and spending £30 or £40 a time on single bets. Boys in the dressing-room would receive tips from 'reliable' sources, but I'd rarely back a winner, so the money wasn't long in drying up. I also liked to put on a fixed-odds football coupon at the weekend. My record at picking a treble was pretty good, and I'd sometimes win around £150 for a £20 stake.

Gambling became another of my growing list of vices, but I suppose it was inevitable I would go the full nine yards – drink, drugs and gambling. Not the ideal pastimes for a professional footballer. It was just typical of the way I lived my life at that time. Typical of the path I was taking on my road to ruin.

During that period, I was hardly paying any attention to Dylan. He was my son, the person who should have come before everyone and everything, and yet he was far too far down my list of priorities. A few bottles of Bud or feeding Dylan his dinner? No contest. A night on the town with some dancing and drugs or playing with Dylan and his toys? Again, no contest.

I was a disgrace as a father. When I think back to the way I behaved, it horrifies me. And I wasn't there often enough for Claire. I should have good memories of being with Dylan, but I really struggle to remember ever changing one of the wee man's nappies. I can't remember telling him a bedtime story. I can't remember picking him up when he fell to comfort him. I can't remember sitting at the dinner table and asking him about his day. I had other priorities – the boozing and partying had taken over my life.

By the middle of the week after a heavy weekend of raving, I'd sometimes wonder if life was worth living. But I didn't go to rave parties every week – it was more like twice a month. I did, however, drink heavily every weekend.

Soon, Ecstasy wasn't enough for me, and I inevitably went in search of a higher high. Cocaine ticked all the boxes. I was right into snorting the stuff by the time I was about 19 and took it regularly until I was caught in an English FA random drugs test when I was at Reading.

A Saturday night would consist of a case of Budweiser. I'd sink

24 bottles without a problem. Beer was my drink, and I'd always take that in preference to spirits. I remember being in the house one Sunday afternoon and drinking a litre bottle of vodka on my own with a coke mixer. I must have downed every last drop in four or five hours. But I didn't feel it was getting me anywhere. I still felt I had no proper alcohol in my system, so I went to the shop and bought myself 12 Budweisers to give me that wee kick I felt was missing. I finished them off in no time and that was me calm and happy.

My drinking was pretty much beyond control by the time I was 20 or 21, but incredibly I still managed to play football, and my career at Dundee United was going well. I was in the first team, and I was able to quite comfortably hide my problem. I wasn't drinking every night at that stage and can put my hand on my heart and say I never, ever got drunk the night before a game. But there were some Friday mornings when I'd go in for training after a heavy one the night before and have to swallow a packet of polo mints before arriving.

A Tuesday night was one of my favourites of the week, as we'd quite often have a Wednesday off. A few of us would head to Grant Johnston's house to play ice hockey on the Sega and have a few beers. Depending on how much we'd had to drink, and if we hadn't been fined in that week's wage packet, we'd play cards for money. The patter was good, and it was a release for most of us. John O'Neil, Duncan Ferguson, Mick O'Neill, Mark Perry, Paddy Connolly, Eddie Conville and Ray McKinnon would usually all be there. We were the regulars of the 'Tuesday Night Club'. I don't know why Grant put up with us. His place was a bombsite by the time we left, yet he'd have it in tip-top condition for us arriving the next time. He was a great host.

I led the way with the drink and would more often than not be the last man standing at the end of the night. However, big Dunc and Eddie always gave me a good run for my money. Wee Paddy was the opposite and was your stereotypical 'two can Dan'.

Sometimes we'd hit the town and go to some of Dundee's hot spots. The Tally-Ho bar was a favourite haunt. Karaoke was the attraction on a Tuesday night, and we'd end up hijacking the microphone. 'American Pie' was our favourite song, but none of us could ever do it justice. The locals put up with us because we played for United, and they liked to see us enjoying ourselves. However, had it been any other bunch of lads, they would have been chased off the stage and barred from the pub.

At that time, I was out of digs and sharing a flat with John O'Neil. John and I got on really well. I'm sure he couldn't have wished for a better person to live with!

John O'Neil: I shared digs with Andy, and it was fine at first, but we got that wee bit older and felt the time was right to move out. We missed the Friday-night phone calls we used to get in the early days. Our digs owner, Tony, would answer the phone and shout, 'John, that's the gaffer for you.'

Wee Jim would be on the other end of the line, and the conversations were, more often than not, bizarre: 'John, this is the gaffer.'

'Hello, gaffer.'

'I'm thinking about playing you tomorrow. Are you confident you'll do well?'

'Aye, gaffer. Of course I am.'

'OK. Now put McLaren on.'

He'd ask Andy the exact same thing. At first, we got quite excited, but in the early days we usually wouldn't even make it onto the bench. He was just keeping us on our toes, maybe hoping that we'd nicked away back down to Glasgow for the night and he'd be gift-wrapped an opportunity to fine us.

Andy was good to share a room with, and we had fun together. Our eating habits were dreadful. We used to stick pies and chips in the deep-fat fryer every night for dinner. I don't even eat chips now, because we all know the importance of a decent diet. Back then, anything went.

Andy's dress sense was appalling. He never used to care what he wore. For a spell, we nicknamed him 'The Ferret' because of this ridiculous bomber jacket he used to wear with a huge sheepskin collar. He just used to laugh it off.

He wasn't laughing when he was on the receiving end of a cracking right hook, though. We were about 19, and there was a young lad on the ground staff called Davie from Blantyre. Andy was always playing pranks on him – the usual stuff, like hiding the boy's clothes and throwing his stuff in the shower. The boy didn't know who it was but was eventually tipped off it was definitely Andy.

A few of us were on the track at Tannadice, and Davie came out with only a towel wrapped around his waist. 'Andy, you better get my stuff out the showers,' he said. 'I know it's been you.'

'Fuck off, wee man. I don't know what you're talking about.'

'Andy, get my stuff now. It's your last chance.'

Again Andy denied it. The next thing we knew, Davie was running at Andy screaming 'Tyre, ya bass', and he lamped him with a brilliant right hook. Andy fell flat on his backside. He came in the next day with an absolute shiner.

It was unusual to see Andy like that. He was always one for thinking that he was more streetwise and harder than the rest of us because he came from Castlemilk. He was his own worst enemy at times for that kind of thing.

Overall, he was a great lad, and I enjoyed my time with him. He certainly made life easier for me to cope with in Dundee. I often felt lonely, but whenever I was down Andy was usually there to lift me back up. He was great company.

We used to look forward to getting down the road at the weekend. Andy wasn't the only one who liked a drink. Knowing I was going back to Dundee on a Monday morning for the start of another long week, I used to love a Sunday night out and would have a decent drink. Andy was also a drinker, but I would say he was more of a binge drinker from my experience of living with him. When he went for it, he really went for it. But it wasn't like he would drink every night.

It was tough being away from home, especially at Dundee United. Yes, most of the players broke through into the first team, but there should have been more to it than that, in my opinion. We were all bored, and it often felt like a prison camp. I remember looking at my pay packet at the end of the financial year, and it had a separate deductions item on it which came to £2,500! Considering we were only on a few hundred quid a week, that was a huge hit to take. We seemed to be fined every other week. Some things were trivial, some not so. Andy, Ray McKinnon, Duncan Ferguson and I seemed to cop it most.

That said, we had some team, and we won the BP Youth Cup three times and the reserve league a few times. We had tremendous pride in our achievements at that level, and every kid who stepped through the front door knew they had a tough job trying to get into the youth team, never mind the reserves or the first team. We were the best at that time, and I think we may well have had the best team at that level in the club's history.

As much as I was playing well and the management were pleased with me, I think I was only performing to about 60 or 70 per cent of what I was capable of because of my drinking. But because I was doing well and holding down a first-team place, there was no need for United to look for reasons as to why I might not be performing to a higher standard.

I thought things on and off the park were going to really improve when Claire and Dylan moved up to Dundee in the early part of 1995. During my previous seven years at United, she had always lived in Glasgow, only occasionally coming up to see me. Most of the time, I would travel down to Glasgow.

We got a nice family home in Monifieth, on the outskirts of Dundee, and it was good to be with Dylan. It should have been the start of something special, and from the outside we must have looked like a normal family. I was earning around £300 a week basic with United at that time and was on an extra £150 if I was playing in the first team. Also, there was a win bonus of up to £600 if we won. On a good week, I was picking up just over £1,000. Happy days.

Claire fell pregnant with Tyler a few months later, and things were good. We were happy to have another baby on the way and delighted for Dylan he was to become a big brother. Tyler was born on 18 November 1996, and he was a big boy, tipping the scales at 10 lb 10 oz. It was great to be blessed with another baby boy. We all had smiles on our faces, but my smile broadened when I had a drink in my hand. After a good session in Dundee on a Saturday night, I'd come home in the early hours and then couldn't wait for morning to come so I could get up and start drinking again. I tried to disguise my drinking in front of Claire by pretending that I wanted to be a good husband and give her a long lie, so I'd get up and sort breakfast and play with Dylan. The real reason I was letting her sleep in was so that I could start drinking. I'd have Budweiser hidden in the house, and by the time she got up in mid-morning I'd have finished half a dozen bottles and be on my way to getting drunk.

As soon as she was up, I'd go to the pub, only planning to have a couple of pints while I watched the football in the afternoon. I would honestly leave the house with the best of intentions of being back in for about five o'clock so we could all sit down together for dinner. Of course, one drink would lead to another, and I'd roll in at about 11 p.m. after the pubs had closed.

I really have no idea why Claire put up with me. I know if the shoe had been on the other foot, I'd have parted company with her. Obviously, she was well aware that I had a drink problem. My mum also knew. I had arguments on several occasions with both of them about it, but it was never something we really spoke about in a controlled manner, never something we sat down together and tried to find a way out of. However, in February 1998, I decided, to an extent, to try to do something about my drinking. I had the best of intentions, but, deep down, I knew I wasn't serious about stopping.

I was in Glasgow and had been out drinking all weekend. I got in the car on Monday morning to drive to Dundee for training, and I smashed it into a lamp post. I'm not sure, but I guess I must have been over the legal limit, as I only managed to drive 50 yards before I lost control. There was a bit of damage done, but it wasn't a write-off. I escaped unhurt, although I was shaken.

I shouldn't have been anywhere near a car – it was one of those days I should have phoned in sick. I wasn't so lucky that morning, but on other occasions I must have had someone up there looking after me. God knows how many times I used to drive back down the road from Dundee after a night on the lash. The next morning, I'd wake up and have no recollection of the 85-mile journey I'd made the night before. I'd look out the window and not believe that my car was parked in the street. On one occasion, I even found a receipt for petrol in the car, as I'd stopped off to fill up on the way down. 'How the hell did I get home last night?' I used to think. When I look back on that period now, I shudder to think what could have happened to me.

But despite my love of drink, I also loved training, and I only called off if I was genuinely ill. When I was in the mood, there was nothing better than being out there with the boys and enjoying a session, whether it be a full-scale practice game or some crossing and finishing.

After my crash, I drove off again and went back to my mum's house. Claire was there. I knew that I had to phone in and tell them I wasn't going to make training that day. Tommy McLean was the manager, and I knew that he'd go off his head, because we weren't getting on well together at that time, so I got my mum to phone in for me. That's how brave I was!

Because of the accident, I was shaking and rattling. My mum was concerned, and I remember saying that I'd be fine if I could get a wee drink to sort me out. It was then, after speaking to

Claire and my mum, that I decided to try and get some help and inform Dundee United that I had a problem. Claire and Mum were keen for me to do it, and I had to be seen to be making an effort for their sakes. To be honest, the main reason I decided to come forward was to try and stop myself from getting a severe verbal beating from McLean and a heavy fine. I also thought that it might get me a couple of days off and give me the chance to calm down and straighten myself out a little bit.

I got the train up to Dundee later that night and reported to Tannadice the next morning. McLean never really spoke to me about what he had been told the previous day, and I was referred to Derek McCormack, the club doctor. I wasn't too honest with him, as I didn't think I had a serious problem. He was keen to help, and I had a lot of time for him. But when a patient isn't forthcoming with information, there's not much he can do. He did give me a telephone number to speak to someone, but I never made the call. To this day, I have no idea who I was supposed to phone or whether it would have been the start of my recovery process.

That said, I stopped drinking for almost three months. Fear kept me away from alcohol. I thought I was on my last legs with Dundee United and that they were watching my every move with a view to getting rid of me. However, the club never followed up my confession to having a drinking problem. I wasn't asked if I was in counselling or addressing the situation properly. To avoid being cornered by McLean, I used to do everything to keep out of his road on a day-to-day basis.

In my personal life, I was worried that Claire was really losing it with me and was at the end of her tether. I should have felt a million dollars, but I actually felt worse. 'Dry drunk' is an expression used in AA, and that's what I was – and a bad one at that. I also thought that I was playing really badly and convinced myself that it was because I wasn't drinking. I was in limbo. When I was off the booze, I should have got in touch with a support network to see what I could do about my problem. But, as I've said, I wasn't ready to fully help myself at that stage of my life. The bottom line was that I was desperate for a drink, and I was just waiting for the ideal opportunity to go on a bender.

The perfect moment arrived near the end of the 1997–98 season when Dundee United avoided relegation in the second-last league game of the season when we played away to Hibs. Our last game of the season was at home to Rangers, and they were going for the championship, so we wanted to secure our safety at Easter Road. Hibs were also in danger of going down, and United offered us a massive financial reward for not losing the game. We were on a bonus of £5,000 for a draw and £10,000 for a win.

It looked grim for us when Grant Brebner gave Alex McLeish's side the lead, but we won 2–1 after our big striker Kjell Olofsson scored a double to keep us in the Premier Division. I was delighted that we'd managed to avoid relegation, and I was overjoyed at picking up £10,000 for a day's work. I went back to the house in Dundee and told Claire that I was going to a supporters' club function to have a couple of drinks to celebrate the result. Claire tried to talk me out of drinking, but I assured her that I was going to take it easy and she had no need to worry. Well, when I left the house I really had no idea what kind of state I was going to get myself into. I wasn't sure if I was going to drink myself into oblivion or just have a few beers.

Thankfully, it was the latter. I went out, enjoyed myself, had fun with the United supporters and only had four or five pints. I came home at a reasonable hour, and I felt good about myself. I thought, 'Ya beauty, I've cracked it.'

A few days later, though, I was back to my old ways when I went on a serious boozing session. I had lots of money in my pocket from the Hibs game, and I just wanted to spend it on drink. I went from bad to worse and ended up out of control that summer. It led to Claire packing her bags and moving back to Glasgow with Dylan and Tyler.

The final straw for her was when Scotland played Brazil in Paris on the opening day of the 1998 World Cup finals. The day before, I had promised Dylan I would take him out to watch the game and spend the full day with him. We'd watch the game, go for a pizza and have a laugh along the way – the kind of day all fathers and sons live for. On the morning of the game, I was getting ready to go out, and I told Claire not to expect me home for dinner, as I was going to meet a few of the boys to watch the match. She started to laugh, thinking that it was a wind-up. 'You're taking Dylan out to watch the game. He's all excited and has hardly slept.' I'd forgotten all about it. The previous night I'd got drunk, and it had gone right out of my head about watching the football with Dylan.

I was faced with a choice: make my boy's day or leave him distraught? Not for the first time, drink won. I'd be able to get a right good booze without Dylan, so I opted to join the boys. I will never, ever forget the look on his face when he found out that I wasn't going to take him. I could see he was really upset – tears were rolling down his cheeks – but being the boy he is he kept saying, 'It's OK, Dad. It's OK.' It was far from OK. It was appalling behaviour.

Thinking about that now leaves me cold and hammers home the point that I put drink before my family. How could any father walk out and leave his son in tears? Of course, I was upset about letting Dylan down but was fine once I had downed a few Buds. There was not an ounce of regret in my body once I was in that 'comfort zone' after a few drinks.

I watched the game and was sorry to see Scotland lose. It would have been terrific for them to get a point against the world champions. I was also really chuffed to see my old Dundee United teammates Darren Jackson and Christian Dailly in the starting line-up for such a memorable occasion.

The day out turned into a right drinking session. I didn't get home until the early hours and woke up with a huge hangover the next morning, which was unusual for me. For all my drinking, I very rarely suffered the following day.

Claire had been left behind to deal with Dylan's disappointment and attempt to sort out yet another mess, and so she quite rightly came into the bedroom and started to shout and bawl at me: 'I can't take it any more, Andy. I'm not going to let you break our hearts any longer. I'm packing my bags and moving back to Glasgow with the boys. You need to take a good look at yourself and decide what you want out of life. Do you want to be a waster for the rest of your days, or do you want to have a decent life with your family?'

I was still too drunk to really take in what she was saying. I think I just pulled the quilt up over my head. I can't remember making any real attempt to talk her round and make her stay. But then she would have known that my words were empty promises. I'd have only said things that I'd never have been able to back up.

Gerry McFadden, Claire's dad, arrived a few hours later. He's a nice guy and didn't give me a hard time, despite what I had been putting his daughter and grandchildren through. However, I went lower in his estimations when I asked him if he could run me to the off-licence so I could get myself a case of Bud. The look on his face said it all.

Claire and the boys left, and I made no attempt to keep them with me. I felt free to go and do whatever I wanted. I lay on the couch and watched the World Cup on the telly. My plan was to fill every spare bit of carpet on the living-room floor with empty Bud bottles. And for the following three days, I gave it one helluva shot. Apart from a couple of packets of crisps and a couple of bars of chocolate, I didn't eat a thing during that 72-hour bender. The only time I moved off the couch was when a taxi arrived at my door to take me for more drink to bring back to the house. I must have drunk close to 150 bottles of Bud. There was hardly a space on the floor – just the way I wanted it.

I went into Dundee at the end of the three days to drink in the pub with the boys, and one of them said to me that I should get a grip because I looked a right mess. I told him to fuck off, because it was the close season and I was entitled to go off the rails.

I don't think I spoke to Claire or my sons during those few days. I eventually phoned her at the end of the week, and I went down to Glasgow to see them. Once again, Claire agreed to patch things up. God knows why, but she always stood by me. She always said that I wasn't a bad person, just easily led.

At the start of the 1998–99 season, I was a total mess. Physically, it was the worse state I'd been in during my whole career. Mentally? Well, I was totally fucked. Paul Sturrock was the manager of United at that point, and he rated me. John Blackley, Sturrock's assistant, was forever telling me that I'd be a star for United if I would just get my head down and be professional. I had ability but lacked the required desire.

By that stage, I didn't even want to play football. I pretended to have a knee injury and refused to train. There was nothing wrong with me, but I had convinced myself that I wasn't fit to play. It was total fantasy. I took it too far, and the club booked me in for an exploratory operation. I allowed myself to be cut open, knowing there wasn't a single thing wrong with me. That's how bad it became for me. It was all to avoid playing football. I'm ashamed of that. I could have been making a contribution or at least making myself available for selection, to justify my wages if nothing else, and I didn't.

My agent was John Viola, and he phoned me to say that Rangers wanted to sign me. The offer came a few months after I had gone in for my fantasy operation. I had managed to get myself back together and was playing football again. I grew up supporting Celtic, but it wouldn't have been a problem signing for Rangers. The chance to win medals, play European football and enhance my bank balance appealed. The only problem was that Dick Advocaat would only take me on a free transfer and that meant I had to wait until my contract expired in November 1999. It was a massive disappointment, and I never got the chance to play in that terrific team alongside such top players as Barry Ferguson, Jörg Albertz, Giovanni van Bronckhorst, Arthur Numan, Rod Wallace and Andrei Kanchelskis. My dad would have been so proud of me. But I had financial problems and couldn't wait seven or eight months to get the move to Ibrox. I was struggling to pay the mortgage and owed a few people money. I was also drinking too much and spent the money for the gas and electricity bills on booze. I needed a serious cash boost to get me out of a hole. I was tempted to wait for Rangers, but I could have broken my leg in the interim and that would have scuppered any transfer.

So, I had to make a decision based on the here and now, and Reading had an offer of around £50,000 for me accepted by Dundee United. I was offered a signing-on fee of £13,000 and close to £1,500 per week in wages. That was brilliant for me, as at that time I was on no more than £400 a week at United. I'd never had a wage like that in my whole life. I thought I'd won the pools.

United were happy to receive some cash for me, so Sturrock sold me, although just three or four years before that move I know that Celtic and Bolton had bids for me of around £500,000 rejected by United. Tommy Burns was manager of Celtic when they tried to buy me, but United refused to sell. Billy Kirkwood was the United gaffer at the time, and I was angry with him and the Tannadice board for denying me the chance to play for my boyhood heroes and to increase my wages. I had my problems at United, but I had given them good service, and they hadn't exactly been paying me top dollar during my time on Tayside.

Tommy Burns: Billy Stark and I wanted to sign a wide player who'd get up and down and get good crosses into the box. Andy was a player we felt met that criteria. He was young, an exciting player and willing to learn. We were playing exciting football at the time and felt Andy would be a good acquisition. But Dundee

United refused to sell. I suppose it made sense for them not to offload one of their best players to Celtic.

I'm sure Andy would have relished the opportunity, and I believe he would have blossomed as a player. Would it have helped his lifestyle off the park? Well, we'll never know.

Andy's loss was young Simon Donnelly's gain. We used Simon in that position, and he ended up getting an extended run in the team and played really well for us.

I'd have loved the chance to play for Celtic, but I'd never have forgiven myself if I had gone there and made a total mess of it. Going to Celtic might have made me clean up my act. On the other hand, earning more money might have made me worse, and I could have ended up going really daft with the drink and drugs.

Joining Reading gave me the chance to eventually team up with Burns. He had big plans for the club and had signed quite a few Scottish boys. So, my new surroundings would include some friendly faces to help me settle in for my first crack at playing down south.

I was delighted to finally get out of Dundee. It gave me some good times but also some depressing memories. I should have left the city sooner and tried something new. However, it was better late than never, and I hoped the move to Reading would signal a change of fortunes for me on and off the park.

It felt strange saying my farewells to the players and staff at Tannadice. I took a few minutes to myself inside the ground and thought of the good times. For example, the pleasure of getting to play a few games alongside a guy such as Dave Narey, a true legend. His nickname was 'Sacha' after the smooth singer Sacha Distel. Dave was a lovely guy and a top player, yet had no ego whatsoever. He was coming to the end of his career as I was starting my involvement with the Dundee United first team, so we mainly played together in reserve games. I used to watch him stroll through matches, and he was never flustered. He has to be one of the finest players ever to have worn the United jersey. I have nothing but respect for him.

I remember being on a boys' night out, and Ray McKinnon had a few drinks down him. He was all over big Sacha: 'You're a legend, big man, a legend.' Dave just stood there with his Black and Tan and smiled. I'm not sure, but I got the impression he never realised just how respected he was and what a great role model he was to Dundee United fans and the young professionals at Tannadice.

Dave was at the heart of the United success story under Jim McLean, but their relationship could be explosive. At the end of one game, I remember Jim ripping Dave apart for his performance. To me, the criticism wasn't justified, and big Dave told the gaffer to fuck off. Jim wasn't having it and told Dave he was fining him. It was ridiculous stuff, and I sat with my head bowed, dying to laugh. A few of the boys felt the same as I did. We couldn't believe two legends were having a barney right in front of us.

As I continued to look back on my career, I shook my head when I remembered the condition I was sometimes in when I arrived for training. Alex Cleland would pick me up faithfully every Monday morning at Bridgeton Cross in Glasgow for the drive back up to Dundee for the start of a new week. Usually, when meeting Alex, I'd fall out of a taxi, hung-over from the night before after yet another marathon session. Alex would also bring me back down the road on a Saturday night, and I'd have a few Buds in the car. I insisted Alex join me, but because he was driving I'd make sure he only had three bottles of Kaliber, non-alcoholic lager. I must have been a total pain in the backside, but Alex never complained.

Apart from being a top-class driver, Alex was also a fine footballer. I'd go as far as to say that he was the best right-back I ever played with. He could play in a variety of positions, but right-back, in my opinion, was where he performed best. He was a professional who never gave a manager a moment of trouble and was completely dependable. He moved to Rangers from Dundee United and played his part in helping the club achieve nine in a row. He then moved to Everton, but injury ended his career prematurely. We still keep in touch, and I will never say a bad word about him.

I also got myself into a few fights at United. As I continued to reminisce, the one with big Sieb Dykstra, our goalie, stood out most. I don't really have much time for keepers, as they can be a strange lot, but I do value their contribution on the pitch and worked beside some top ones, including Alan Main and Gordon Marshall. Physically, Sieb was a giant of man, and he was good at collecting cross balls. He used to love coming off his line. He might not always take the ball, but he'd come nevertheless! He was a confident keeper and pulled off some great saves. I think the sheer size of him also used to intimidate opposition players.

Mentally, though, he could be weak. He would always take the bait and was easy to wind up. I used to torture him every day about his big, porno-style moustache and tell him that his wife had him under her thumb. He didn't take kindly to either. One day, on the way to an away game, I was sleeping at the back of the bus, and he poured water over me. I had a bottle of Lucozade and threw it all over him. He went nuts and attacked me. It was like Frazier v. Ali! We were pulled apart by Steven Pressley, and I taunted Sieb, saying, 'Is that your best shot, big man?' To be honest, I thought he was going to give me a tanking. Mark Perry was sitting next to me, and he curled up into a ball, shitting himself. Thanks for your help, Mark! Tommy McLean was the manager at the time, and he was at the front of the bus, pissing himself laughing.

I also thought back to some of the laughs we had enjoyed and remembered that nine times out of ten Duncan Ferguson had been at the centre of them. On the pitch, Big Dunc must have been a nightmare for defenders to play against. I'd go so far as to say that he was sometimes unplayable. He was quick, strong and good in the air. He could also score goals. I remember one game we played against Aberdeen, and he jumped *higher* than the crossbar to score with a header. He moved from United to Rangers and then to Everton and Newcastle and back to Everton. I couldn't believe it when Dunc was banged up in jail after an incident with Jock McStay when he was playing for Rangers against Raith Rovers. Some of the publicity he received was just not the Dunc I knew. He was portrayed as a bit of a nutter, yet I only knew him as being a top-class footballer and, more importantly, an absolute gentleman.

We grew up together at United, and the young boys at Tannadice all made sure we looked out for each other. We were like a little family. When we were a wee bit older at United and new kids arrived at the club, Dunc was extremely generous to them. He made sure that they were never short of a few quid and would have given away his last penny. He was lively in the dressing-room but could sometimes be a touch unpredictable. One day, we were travelling from his house in Stirling up to Dundee, and he let a couple of pigeons go halfway through the journey. He loved his birds and really took his pigeon keeping seriously. Before letting them fly off, he whispered something to them and then opened the window. I don't know where they were supposed to be heading or if they made it, but Dunc appeared to have every confidence they'd eventually find their way home.

Dunc had a terrific career but would have achieved so much more had it not been for serious injuries. I've not spoken to him for years but know that if I picked up the phone to the big man we'd be able to chat away as if we'd never been apart. As far as I'm concerned, he is still the Dunc I knew from our days in Dundee more than 16 years ago. The only difference is that he will have several more zeros in his bank account now, and good luck to him for working hard to achieve his fortune. He deserves every penny.

I picked up a few grand in bonus money the night we defeated Partick Thistle in the Premier League play-off game in May 1996. The first leg was at Firhill, and we fell behind to an Andy Lyons goal in the first half. Christian Dailly equalised for us with just four minutes left when he got on the end of a Dave Bowman cross and powered a header past Nicky Walker, who had pulled off some incredible saves that afternoon. That was a vital goal, and I felt it was the turning point in the tie. We were the First Division side trying to get back up in one season, and we had a squad good enough to do it. The team included Craig Brewster, Steven Pressley, Robbie Winters, Owen Coyle and Gary McSwegan – all Premier League standard. The second leg was on a Thursday night and Tannadice was packed. We had lots of pressure but fell behind in the 72nd minute when Ian Cameron scored from the penalty spot. We looked dead and buried until I sent over a cross and big Brian Welsh was there to score with a header.

I felt good that night. I was right up for the game, as there was no way I fancied another season in the First Division. I gave the Thistle defence a hard time. In fact, it was probably my most productive game for United. I was really chuffed to set up the extra-time winner for Coyle. I chased a long pass and probably had no right to reach it, especially at that time of the game when I'd run my backside off, but I found the energy from somewhere and sent a ball over for Coyle to sidefoot home. The game was won.

Owen Coyle: Andy is one of the most talented individuals I ever played with. Pace, good with either foot and great composure in front of goal. His performance that night was as good as any I've ever seen from a wide player in my whole career. When he set me up for my goal, he just lifted his head and picked me out. He put the correct pace on the cross, and all I had to do was guide the ball past Nicky Walker.

To win promotion was so important to United that season. It would have been catastrophic not to get back up, and there's no doubt Andy has to take as much credit as anyone for getting the club back into the top flight. If we hadn't defeated Partick Thistle, then who knows how long it might have taken to get back up. If you don't do it at the first attempt, then it tends to set you back, and it can mean a three- or four-year wait.

Andy and I travelled up together from Glasgow to Dundee, along with Robbie Winters. I honestly had no idea he had a problem with alcohol. He was always bubbly and good company.

We were back in the Premier League, and I was delighted for our fans and the gaffer Billy Kirkwood. If only all my Tannadice memories were as good. I was happy to get out of Tannadice when I did. I suppose it would have better if it had been sooner. Moving to Reading should have been the start of a new, positive chapter in my life. But it wasn't. Up until then, my decline as a footballer had been a gradual process over a period of years. Now, though, moving to England was the start of a rapid decline as drink and drugs took over completely.

Paul Sturrock: When I came back to United as manager, I could immediately tell that Andy was a different man to the one I'd left behind a few years earlier when I went to St Johnstone. He was a spent force. He no longer had a great engine and his sharpness had gone. His overall fitness had deteriorated. The drink had clearly taken over. I tried to get him back together and reinvigorate him. I often pulled him into my office and tried to get him to put things back together, but he was not listening. He was not acknowledging what was happening to him.

All sorts of stories were doing the rounds in Dundee about him, and we had to act. Some of the stories were rubbish and some were accurate. But you can't keep an eye on a player 24 hours a day. In the end, I had to move Andy on. It was best for Dundee United and for him.

I knew he hadn't earned big money at United, and the chance to go to Reading allowed him to make a few quid. I was happy to let him go and thought that getting away from Dundee and being away from Glasgow would benefit him.

Overall, I had many unhappy times at United, but also many good times, and none more so than when we won the Scottish Cup in 1994.

6

LIFTING THE CUP IN '94

I HOPE the SFA don't haul me up, or the police come knocking at my door, but when I was a kid I used to 'break in' to Hampden Park with my mates and play on the hallowed turf. I was about 11 or 12 at the time, and we would sneak in during the summer holidays. I used to love being off school for the whole of July and half of August. By that point in my life, education had simply became an inconvenience to me. I was always desperate to hear the school bell ring at four o'clock to signal home time. And home time for me meant football time.

Through the mists of time, it's easy to reflect on childhood and only remember the good times. I always recall the sun splitting the sky, darkness not falling until after ten and staying out all day playing football with my mates. I'd get out of bed early and only return to the house for something to eat. I'd grab a sandwich and a drink of juice at lunchtime, and in the evening I'd scoff my tea as quickly as possible so that I could get out to play with my pals again. When we went away on a summer holiday, I'd enjoy it, but, ultimately, I was itching to get back to Castlemilk to play football with my pals.

Football, undoubtedly, was all I wanted to do, which is the same for most young boys brought up on a scheme, I'm sure. We'd play games on the local red-ash pitches, and if we were lucky we'd sometimes get to use a spare bit of grass. It was great fun until some busybody with nothing better to do with their day than ruin kids' pleasure came along, pointed to the 'No Ball Games' sign and tried to chase us away. Often, we'd just refuse to leave and innocently claim we weren't doing any harm. It was a different matter when the police turned up, though. I always thought that they were reluctant to chase us on, because we weren't really doing any harm. The opposite, in fact: we were staying out of trouble and doing something that kept us fit. But sadly for us, the police had to be seen to be following the letter of the law. And people wonder why there's a shortage of footballing talent coming through the ranks. What chance have you got when kids are being restricted from playing the game?

Undeterred, we looked for alternatives, and one day one of the boys came up with the idea of going to Hampden. Me, Rocky, Eddie, Davie and Alan walked the mile along Aikenhead Road and onto the grounds of the national stadium for a look around. After some investigative work, we found a wee gap in a fence at the traditional 'Celtic End' of the ground, and we were in. Back then, the ground wasn't all-seated, and we ran down the steps of the terracing and onto the pitch. There was no one around to stop us, and we couldn't believe our luck.

We played wee games of three a side or 'two 'n' in'. It was such an exhilarating feeling to have the freedom to play on that pitch. I'd take turns at pretending which player I was. Some days I'd be Kenny Dalglish and other times I'd be Charlie Nicholas. I'd score a goal and then run away with my arms in the air, imagining 60,000 Celtic fans were chanting my name because I'd won the cup for their club.

We weren't just content with playing on the pitch. After the game, we would go through the motions of climbing up the stairs into the main stand as if we were receiving the cup. We used to hold up our ball, a hand clasped on either side of it, and shake it about with sheer pleasure. We convinced ourselves that it was the Scottish Cup we were holding aloft.

Every May, I watched the Scottish Cup final on television. Back then, hardly any live games were shown on the box, and so it was a big day in front of the telly. If you weren't at the game, every father and son would be in the house together watching the showpiece event of the football season. I'd have my bottle of Irn-Bru and sweets, and I'd really enjoy the build-up to the game, the match, and the interviews and laps of honour afterwards.

One game that sticks in my mind is the 1980 Scottish Cup final when Celtic beat Rangers 1–0 thanks to a George McCluskey goal. Of course, that game is infamous because of the running battles between the fans on the pitch after the final whistle and the subsequent alcohol ban at football grounds across the country.

I genuinely used to dream about being involved in a cup final and was privileged to do so on 21 May 1994 when Dundee United played against Rangers. We had a bit of a rocky run in getting there and came close to going out on a couple of occasions. We defeated Arbroath 3–2 away in the third round on a freezing cold and windy day at Gayfield. Scott Crabbe, Craig Brewster and Billy McKinlay scored for us that day, but Arbroath made it difficult and pulled it back to 3–2 to make the final 13 minutes quite nervy. We were home to Motherwell in the next round and drew 2–2. We were ahead thanks to a double from Brewster. But John Philliben scored in injury time to force a replay. We won the second game at Fir Park 1–0. Big Brian Welsh scored the goal with a brilliant shot from the edge of the box. Airdrie were next up in the quarter-final tie, and we drew 0–0 with them at Broomfield. Brewster was sent off by referee Andrew Waddell in that game, and most observers agreed both yellow cards were harsh.

Up until that point, I wasn't involved in any of the cup games. I can't remember why I was out of the team, but I'd guess a mixture of loss of form and some disciplinary matters may well have been at the heart of it all. However, United gaffer Ivan Golac named me as a sub for the replay against Airdrie at Tannadice, and I came on after eight minutes to replace the injured Jerren Nixon. Six minutes later, I scored our opener when I hit a shot from about fifteen yards past John Martin. The Airdrie keeper was on a great run at the time, and it was the first goal he'd conceded in 461 minutes of football. McKinlay scored our second goal, and that took us through to the semi-final.

I felt great that night. It was important that I played well to send a message to Golac I was ready to play a major part in the final two months of the season.

Aberdeen were our semi-final opponents, and we drew 1–1 at Hampden in front of a crowd of just under 22,000, which was a disappointing turnout. Duncan Shearer gave Aberdeen the lead in the seventh minute, and we scored through big Welsh in the last minute when he headed home Dave Bowman's cross. A last-minute leveller may sound lucky, but the truth is that we should have had the game won before then. John Burridge pulled off an incredible save to stop me scoring the opener with a header, and then I hit a post with another header later on. The goal we conceded was soft, as Guido van de Kamp should have prevented it from going in. So, we felt disappointed not to have got it done and dusted at the first attempt.

The replay was played in front of a crowd of less than 14,000 – very poor for what should have been a showpiece occasion. But that didn't matter to us in the end, as we won the game through Jim McInally's goal in the 70th minute. Dons keeper Theo Snelders couldn't hold Dave Bowman's shot, and Jim smashed in the rebound. We were on our way to the cup final, where we would face Rangers.

We stayed at a hotel in East Kilbride the night before the final. I think it was called the Westpoint Hotel at the time, but it has changed its name several times since then. Typically, Golac encouraged a relaxed atmosphere as we prepared for our big day. There was a horse-racing meeting on at Hamilton on the Friday afternoon, and he allowed a few of the boys to go along and unwind. He also told us that it was fine to have a couple of pints in the hotel bar to help us relax. We were all quite surprised and couldn't believe we were being allowed a bevvy. For me, being told by the gaffer that I was allowed alcohol was the last thing I needed to hear. Having a couple of pints would just have frustrated me. Now, if Golac had said, 'Lads, go to the bar and drink the place dry,' then I'd have been first up and wouldn't have budged until it was time to board the bus for Hampden, but getting a wee taste of a drink and then having to stop would have driven me up the wall. So, I resisted the temptation, as did the rest of the boys.

Back then, *Sportscene* always made a big deal of cup-final day and had a special programme on the Friday night, in which they broadcast live from our hotel. The place was buzzing, and a few of the boys and the manager gave interviews. I shunned the limelight that night and watched it from my hotel room with a couple of the lads. We kept noticing Mark Perry popping up in the background of every camera shot, and some of the boys eventually went downstairs to slaughter him!

On the day of the game, Golac's team talk was all about our strengths and what we could do to Rangers. He never really went into detail about them and never highlighted anything we should be wary of. We were all very relaxed, and that calmness stemmed from the manager. I had a feeling we would win and went into the final with an enormous amount of self-belief.

In the final 15 minutes leading up to kick-off, Maurice Malpas had a blether with me and said I should enjoy the occasion to the full. 'Make the most of today, Andy,' he said. 'Savour every moment and don't come off the park with any regrets. You never know when you'll get another opportunity like this.'

Of course, I was my usual cocky self. I was just 20 and had already played in the Under-16 World Cup final for Scotland at Hampden in front of more than 50,000 fans. 'This is going to be the first of many Scottish Cup finals for me,' I thought as Maurice said his piece. 'I've got another 15 years to play and be involved in occasions like this.'

Rangers were truly an outstanding side during that period. They had quality players and a tremendous will to win. The previous year they had just failed to reach the final of the European Cup, and they hoped to secure back-to-back Trebles by beating us in the final. According to many observers, it was the finest Rangers team for more than 20 years. So, we were massive underdogs, but the gaffer never at any point made us feel inferior.

I got the nod to play ahead of Jerren Nixon. I was suspended for the final two league games of the season and knew my starting slot in the final was in jeopardy. However, in our final league game of the season, we lost 3–0 at home to Raith Rovers. I watched from the stand that day and must have been one of the very few people who left Tannadice smiling. I knew the performance was rotten and the manager would have to make changes. And I was right. I was in and Nixon was on the bench.

We played well that day, and I reckon we deserved to win. Brewster scored the winner in 47 minutes after a bit of a mix up between Rangers keeper Ally Maxwell and Dave McPherson. It was a magical moment. It was the first time in United's history that we'd managed to lift the cup. Nobody can ever take that away from any of the boys who played that day. It was a little piece of history. We were legends – each and every one of us. Dave Narey, Paul Hegarty and Paul Sturrock achieved so much with United but couldn't get that elusive Scottish Cup victory, which made me appreciate all the more just what a fantastic thing we'd achieved. In a strange way, it didn't feel right that I had won the cup at just 20 when these guys had given so much in the competition and hadn't ever won it.

I was pleased for big Gordan Petric, who played well that day. He was always a rock – different class. He was as strong as an ox and had the body strength to hold off any opponent. He also took no bull from anyone and was a great guy to have on your side. He was my man of the match that day, as he made sure the likes of Ally McCoist, Gordon Durie and Duncan Ferguson didn't get a sniff.

Like so many United players, he moved to Rangers, but it never really worked out for him there. Big Gordan also had a bit of a mad streak and would do things that only he thought were funny. However, if you were on the receiving end of his 'joke', you would see it differently. For example, he had hands like shovels and used to grab your shoulders and then squeeze until you had lost your breath. He used to laugh, but I failed to see the funny side, as it was agony. Still, Gordan is the kind of guy I'd have with me in the trenches any day of the week.

At the final whistle, I went to celebrate with Christian Dailly, and I remember looking up to see Claire and my mum in the stand. I was delighted to see them happy, and I was also pleased for the gaffer. Golac was unpredictable and totally different from Jim McLean. Hardly anyone reckoned he would achieve anything at United, and he never really helped his cause by sometimes making ludicrous statements to the media. Some people believed he was a bit of a joke figure, but he got it spot on for the cup final, and he will be fondly remembered at United.

Golac took over from McLean, and for all the success Jim had at United – a league championship and a UEFA Cup final – incredibly he lost five Scottish Cup finals. I was the first player to see him after the final whistle and, for once, he was genuinely pleased. Yet he couldn't help himself, and in typical wee Jim fashion said, 'That Craig Brewster has cost this club a lot of money today.' He had a smile on his face when he said it, so I presume he was being sarcastic. He was referring to the £6,000 bonus we were all on to win the cup, and it had been mentioned by a couple of the players that they'd heard Craig was on a personal bonus if he scored 20 goals that season. His winner that day was his 20th of the campaign.

I walked up the stairs to receive my medal. I'd had some practice from my days 'breaking in' to Hampden as a schoolboy, but this time it was for real. I was fourth in line. Naturally, as captain, Maurice was first. Gary Bollan was next, followed by Jim McInally. It was my turn after him. Don't ask me why I can remember those details.

As I made my way up the stairs, I was laughing to myself. No one knew why, but it was because my dad was a massive Rangers fan, and I thought of him watching the game from his place of rest. He used to watch Rangers all the time, and seeing us defeat his side that day must have been awkward for him. Still, I'm sure he'd have been chuffed for me and would have wanted us to win the game. I was gutted he wasn't there.

I received my medal and waited for the rest of the lads to do the photographs for the Sunday papers and then go on our lap of honour. I reckon my circuit must have been the quickest in the history of any winning team. I must have had it done and dusted inside a minute. There were joyous scenes all around us as the United fans partied in the stands, but I couldn't really care less. All I wanted was to escape the limelight and get inside the dressing-room to get stuck into the booze. I knew there would be loads of drink waiting for us, and I wanted to be the first to get my hands on it. Not even a Scottish Cup triumph could stop me from wanting a drink.

But before heading back to the dressing-room, I had one thing to do and that was go over and wave to a wee girl who used to go to all of our games. She'd always unfurl a banner which had 'Andy, my hero' written on it, so I got into a routine of waving to her before games, and now and again I'd give her a wee hug. It became a sort of a good-luck thing. That day, I waved to her and then walked off the park.

Now, I wish I had stayed out there and savoured the moment more, just as Maurice Malpas had said to me. But I was first in and immediately got wired in. Heaven. I opened a can of lager and went into the bath with my full kit on. I guzzled a few beers and some champagne and was having a great time of it. We also had to get jabs that day for our trip to Trinidad and Tobago the next week. I hate jabs and have a real fear of needles. Maybe that's why I was eager to get so drunk after the game – I wanted to numb the pain!

I went for a bevvy with my mates from Castlemilk after the game. First, I stood outside Hampden and snapped a couple of photos with Claire and my mum. I then handed Claire my strip and medal and told her to look after them. I just wanted to get away from Hampden as quickly as possible so I could go on a bender with my mates. The team bus left without me and headed back up to Dundee for the celebrations. I can't remember if I was given permission to stay local for a few hours or if they just didn't notice I wasn't on the bus.

Anyway, a few boozers beckoned, and I was in my element. I was the centre of attention and didn't need to put my hand in my pocket all night. One of the boys stayed sober and drove us up to Dundee a few hours later. He must have had to stop every two minutes to let me out for a pee. Dundee United supporters buses passed us on the A9 and all tooted their horns when they recognised me.

I'd booked a room at the Stakis Hotel in Dundee that night, because it was my intention to be there for the party and for the open-top bus parade around Dundee on the Sunday afternoon. As usual, I took things too far when I got back to Tayside. I was well gone with the drink, and the hotel security would not let me in the front door to go to the United function because they didn't recognise me. One of the United lads had to come and sort it all out. I then got stuck into the booze and had a great night.

I woke up the next morning still wearing my clothes from the previous night. I headed downstairs for some breakfast, and all the players were there, showered and shaved, looking immaculate for the big day. I looked like a bag of shit. I could sense a few of them looking at me and no doubt a few shook their heads. They were probably quite right.

The married players had their wives with them and the others had their girlfriends. But Claire was down the road in Glasgow looking after Dylan. I didn't invite either of them. It's selfish things like that that now make me angry with myself. However, my biggest regret is that Dylan was not at the game. He should have been there. And he and Claire should have been at the celebration party and then on the open-top bus.

After breakfast, the players went to get ready for the reception and tour through Dundee. I headed straight to the bar and downed a couple of Buds. I then stuffed bottles of lager into my pockets for the afternoon parade, because the thought of going a couple of hours without a beer filled me with dread.

The bus picked us up at the hotel, and we drove into the heart of Dundee. The whole place was awash with tangerine. There must have been at least 30,000 people lined up along the streets, hanging from windows and on rooftops. I recognised some of the fans, and it made me feel proud to see them so happy at our achievement. Winning the cup meant so much to some that they were in tears. Some of those I spoke to afterwards were genuinely overcome, and it hammered home what it was all about when they said things like, 'This is the happiest day of my life, son.'

The parade came to a climax at the Lord Provost's office in the main square, and we all took a turn going out onto the balcony – well, it was more like a ledge – with the cup. It was a great feeling.

I got totally blitzed, and much of that day, like the night before, was lost in a haze of alcohol. However, I've never watched a rerun of the cup final. I rarely look back and try not to dwell on the past, especially on good things. The way I like doing it is to play games back in my head. And then I tend to be negative about my performance. After the cup final win against Rangers, a boy in the pub said to me, 'You were brilliant today, Andy,' but I was critical of myself. It was the same old story – I was never positive about anything.

However, when I think back to it now, I know that I *did* play well. I was on the left wing and was up against Gary Stevens, who was an England international. I was doing fine, and then Gary got injured. Neil Murray replaced him, and I caused him problems all afternoon. Rangers then adjusted their tactics and moved Ian Ferguson over to the right to help keep me in check. That was a huge compliment. I got a couple of really good crosses in that day. I was taken off with nine minutes to go but had made a good contribution to our win.

But it's in the past, and I rarely think back to it. My medal and jersey are somewhere in Claire's gran's house. I'm hopeless with things like that. I really should have my strip framed and let the boys decide where in the house it should hang, but I haven't. Maybe we'll do that one of these days.

Maurice Malpas: Andy was always involved in daft stuff but never anything nasty. One thing that sticks out for me about him was the day a woman from the local drugs-awareness programme visited Tannadice to speak to the youth players. The agency visited the club once or twice a year. I was helping out with the coaching of the youth team at that time and attended the meeting. The woman pulled out a clear bag, threw a load of tablets onto the table and asked if anyone in the room could tell her what they were. Andy was first on his feet and went through almost every tablet, explaining what they were used for. There was an Ecstasy tablet, and Andy went into detail about that one and others. He also educated the group on how the police would deal with you if you were caught in possession of certain drugs. He knew the lot. He was about 17 at the time, and I was totally astounded by his knowledge. He was streetwise. I was married with kids and didn't have a clue about that side of life. He was more than ten years younger than me and knew all there was to know about it. I'll never forget that day.

As a footballer, Andy was blessed with natural talent and very good pace. He just didn't use it properly. I felt his biggest problem was that he lacked concentration. He never seemed to be able to take everything in and then put it all to use. I think his mind was too busy wandering, thinking about what he was going to get up to at the weekend or what he had just been up to the night before.

He'd have a good game on a Saturday and then live on that performance for the next two or three weeks, whereas he should have been building on that to take him on a run of eight or nine good games in a row.

Because of the way he led his life during the week, his preparation for games wasn't good enough, and there's no doubt his form suffered. He could drink crates of lager without any problem. He missed many Monday-morning training sessions because of being on the drink at the weekend. His body took too much abuse for there to have been no comeback. He didn't like the discipline we had at United and was too immature to appreciate it was for his own good. At the end of the day, rules were in place to help the club win football games and for the players to maximise their potential and talent.

If Andy hadn't drank to excess, then I've no doubt he would have reached the very top level and stayed there for a few years. But he liked to drink and liked to drink far too much. When he was on the drink, he would usually become a pest and get louder and louder. He wasn't a bad person, and despite coming from Castlemilk, as he used to like to remind everyone, he couldn't fight sleep whether he was drunk or sober.

I've also got two runners-up medals from my career. One is from the 2001 League Cup final when I played for Kilmarnock and we lost to Celtic. I was a sub that day, and the phenomenal Henrik Larsson scored a hat-trick. My other medal came from the 1997–98 League Cup final when Dundee United lost 3–0 to Celtic at Ibrox. I was actually suspended for that game, as I had picked up two bookings in the competition. My second yellow card came in the semi-final against Aberdeen at Tynecastle when Hugh Dallas booked me.

I wasn't in the mood for attending the final, as I was gutted at missing out. When I'm in that frame of mind, I'm not a good spectator, but I was more or less forced to go, because Tommy McLean, United's manager at that time, and the players wanted me to be involved in some capacity. I was in the dressing-room before the game, and Steven Pressley asked me if I was OK. He must have sensed that I was really down, but I put a brave face on it and pretended to be fine.

We conceded two goals quite early on, and I just wanted to get away from my seat in the stand and into the players' lounge for a booze. I couldn't even wait until half-time. I think I made my way to the bar after about 25 minutes and pestered a woman behind the counter to give me a bottle of beer. I gave her my best smile, and she eventually served me, although she wasn't supposed to until half-time. I ended up downing a right few more, and before the final whistle I was well on my way to being sozzled. That's just the way life was for me at that time.

During the following week, McLean pulled me into his office and gave me a medal that one of the Swedish boys at the club had handed in. McLean thought I should I get it, and it was nice of him to think of me. I didn't really want it, but he persuaded me to take it. I gave that one and the one from my cup final with Kilmarnock to my sons to play with. I don't know where the medals are now. I should have taken more care of them.

God, you'd think I had a hundred of them from my career. Still, I'm so proud of my 1994 Scottish Cup winners' medal.

7

READING

I MOVED to Reading when I was twenty-five at the start of what should have been the best six or seven years of my career. The transfer fee they paid should have gone down in their history books as one of their finest pieces of business, instead it ended up being one of their biggest wastes of money.

If I had serious intentions of giving it a proper go, I would have bought a family home and moved Claire and the boys down. That's what most footballers do, isn't it? Move their nearest and dearest as soon as they can to help them settle in and embrace the local community. I was earning enough money to buy a nice property in somewhere like Newbury in Berkshire. But that was never my intention. I was happy for Claire to be up the road and out of sight so she could not see how far I was letting myself go. Being down there on my own and seeing her every weekend or second weekend meant I had the best of both worlds.

Tommy Burns was my gaffer at Reading. He's a terrific guy, and I wanted to do well for him. However, at that point in my life, nothing or no one got the better of the drink. Tommy had great ideas for the club and was passionate about his job there. He just didn't get the results he needed, and I don't believe he always enjoyed a smooth working relationship with club owner John Madejski. Tommy was criticised for some of his signings and things just never got going the way he wanted.

I know I could and should have contributed much more to Reading. The club had an excellent 25,000 all-seater stadium that generated a decent atmosphere. But, most of the time, I found it hard to turn it on for them. In some of the games, my performances were not up to the required standard. I soon realised that I could no longer drink heavily during the week then produce the goods on a match day. My body had had enough of being neglected, and it was starting to wear itself down. At that stage of my life, after years of abusing my body and mind, I had to make a choice – either get help to tackle my addictions to drink and drugs or keep going, in which case I knew I would be lucky to still be in the professional game in one year's time. Not surprisingly, the vices won.

I was already familiar with a few players at Reading. Tommy had signed a few Scotsmen, and guys such as Jim McIntyre, Scott Howie, Stuart Gray and Grant Brebner had already been there for a year or so by the time I arrived. They knew their way about Reading and could point me to the kind of haunts I wanted. That was, basically, anywhere that sold alcohol.

I soon got to know a couple of pubs in the area, but most of the time I was happy to drink in the hotel the club had put me up in for the first three months of my stay in Reading. Most of the time I'd put everything on the tab, and at the end of the week the bill would get sent back to the club, as I had it in my deal that all food and drink expenses would be paid for during my stay in the hotel. I'd often drink the mini-bar in my room dry of Bud then go to the bar downstairs and order more. The hotel barman came from Dumbarton and was a Celtic supporter, so we used to spend a lot of time together. One night, we were chatting, and he told me that since I'd checked in to the hotel the management had increased their order of Bud from two cases a week to five. At the time, I was quite proud of that fact. That's how sick I was.

I was pretty much out of control. The bottom line was I was throwing away my career, but I couldn't have cared less. Saturday night was my favourite time of the week. When we played at home, I would rush to the airport to get the last flight to Glasgow. My motivation for being eager to return north should have been to spend time with Claire and the boys, but that wasn't what it was about for me.

I'd fly business class, which meant I got access to a lounge at the airport. The drink was all free, and I'd sink as many beers as possible before I boarded the flight. Most of the people in the lounge were respectable and would sit with a coffee or one or two drinks. Not me. I'd be in there in my Reading tracksuit well on my way to getting pissed.

I'd phone Claire just before boarding to make sure that she'd got a crate of Bud for my return home. It was never about asking how she or the kids were or what kind of day she'd had. It never entered my head to ask if she wanted to go out for a meal or go to the pictures. It was always all about me – all about satisfying my need for a drink. She'd had the boys all week and should have looked forward to me getting back so that we could spend quality time together as a family and as a couple. But I never gave Claire that. I'd just want to have a few drinks and then catch up with my pals.

My return flight back was usually early on a Monday morning, and it was a struggle to get out of bed and make it to the airport, as I would have had such a heavy couple of nights previously. To be honest, by the time I joined Reading, every morning was becoming more of a struggle. I only wanted to get out of bed to get a drink. During my days at United, I'd never had a problem getting out of bed for training, no matter how hard I'd partied the night before. I always enjoyed going to training and putting in a shift. But that was no longer the case. I looked on football as a job, something I had to do in order to pick up a wage rather than something I enjoyed. There was no longer any fun in it for me.

Reading were good to me and didn't deserve to have a player with such disrespect for them on their books. When I signed, they were in the old English Second Division. It was a really tough league with the likes of Fulham, Manchester City, Preston and Wigan all trying to move up into the First Division.

My debut was at home against Manchester City on 27 March 1999, and we lost 3–1. My next home game was against Fulham. Kevin Keegan was their manager at the time, and I played against Philippe Albert. We lost 1–0. I found those games a bit of a struggle, because I wasn't fit enough and I was drinking too much. Yet I always thought that I was better than the Second Division. I still looked upon myself as the player I had been two or three years before when Celtic and Bolton had tried to sign me. Not long before I joined Reading, Preston boss Davie Moyes asked me down for a week to look at me, and I was set to go on a Monday morning. Stupidly, I got drunk at the weekend and never made it down. Again, my no-show at Deepdale was down to me thinking I was better than that standard. United were furious I didn't show up, as they were desperate to sell me.

I knew I had to get out of Dundee. I reckoned a move would see me calm down my drinking, or 'screw the nut' as I used to call it. But, if truth be told, there was never any serious intent on my part to try to stop completely. I got to know local boys in Reading that weren't involved in the game. They'd go out drinking for most of the day, and I was happy to join them. I used to ask the lads in the dressing-room if any of them wanted to join me for an afternoon session to calm my nerves. Most days, I'd end up in the pub from about two in the afternoon until closing time. Nine hours solid bevvying.

In my second month at Reading, I found my touch and I was flying. So much so that I was awarded the Player of the Month award from the local paper. Wigan had beaten us 4–1 early in the season, but I'd scored our goal. I felt good about my game and was starting to find a bit of a rhythm.

I remained in the hotel until the end of the season. Claire and the boys came down one weekend to visit, and we all had a great time. I thought then about asking her to move down permanently but soon realised it would be a bad idea. She'd have been nearly 500 miles from Glasgow and would have needed proper love and support to make it worth her while, but I knew I couldn't give her and the boys that.

I was back in a hotel for the start of pre-season in early July. Reading no longer paid for my stay, but I managed to wangle a deal for about £25 per night bed and breakfast. When I signed for the club, part of my deal was a £10,000 relocation fee. Most players use this to pay for the legal fees when buying and selling property as they move from one city to another. My £10,000 was spent in a few months on booze and, latterly, paying my hotel bills.

I was drinking heavily, but my football was going well. We beat Bristol City 2–1 on the opening day of the new season, and Burns gave me the Man of the Match award. At that time, Tommy had a wee joke going and gave the best player a Mars bar as a reward. Well, better to give me that than a bottle of champagne!

We then had a game on a Tuesday night early in the season against Peterborough in the League Cup. I lasted about an hour and came off with a tight hamstring. I told Tommy I was fine for the following Saturday, but he was having none of it. He said there was no way I was ready to play four days later if I had a genuine hamstring injury. There's no doubt Tommy had tippled to my off-the-field problems.

I was drinking heavily every day, apart from the night before a game. Most mornings I would get a chap at the door at about eight o'clock, and there'd be a girl there with a cooked breakfast for me. I'd have no recollection of ordering it the night before. When I was on the drink, I never had anything in the morning apart from a glass of juice. I must have gone to bed pissed feeling hungry, thinking I'd want the 'works' when I woke up. Since I've been sober, I eat toast or cereal every morning. If I don't, I get dizzy spells at training.

I eventually moved out of the hotel a few weeks into the start of the season, but I didn't even bother getting my own place. My teammate Jimmy Crawford lived alone and said I could move in with him. That was the start of Jimmy's downfall at the club. He was a really nice lad, and I wish he'd never got involved with me.

It wasn't just ordering food I couldn't remember. I'd phone Claire in the afternoon and apologise for not getting in touch the previous night, but she'd tell me we'd been on the phone to each other for an hour. I'd never had blackouts before. I was also starting to suffer from hangovers, and that's when it became a problem to get out of bed. I was dying in the mornings, and I used to have to talk to myself to get up. 'Come on, Andy,' I'd say. 'Have a shower, get through the next couple of hours and then settle yourself down with a couple of pints in the afternoon.'

I wasn't the only guy suffering. Results were not good, and Tommy was sacked in September 1999. I felt sorry for him, I really did. There's no doubt I let him down. I phoned him up a few months after I'd sobered up and apologised for my lack of professionalism at Reading. Typically, though, Tommy didn't hold any grudges. He didn't want me to blame myself for anything and told me not to worry about it. Instead, I was to make sure I stayed on the straight and narrow and worked hard to get my life and career back on track.

Tommy was aware I had a problem. A couple of the players called a meeting in the first-team dressing-room, but I'm sure it was at Tommy's behest. The meeting was mainly about the discipline of the squad and our drinking habits, but I got the feeling it was aimed mainly at me. Barry Hunter, one of my teammates, accused me of having a drink problem. I denied it, and there was nothing he could do about it.

Tommy Burns: I knew Andy was experiencing difficult times off the park at Dundee United, and his reputation was growing for that kind of thing. You do your homework on potential signings, and after speaking to a few people I thought he would be fine if he had a change of environment. Also, we were getting him for about £50,000, so it wasn't a gamble from that point of view.

It soon became apparent Andy was in trouble and unable to help himself. I was getting feedback from the hotel and one or two other sources about his drinking, and I was concerned. We were also concerned about one or two other players at the club, and we organised for some tests to be carried out. The results that came back meant we had to keep a close eye on Andy. However, at no point did I ever think he looked completely done in.

He continued to slip away after my time at Reading was at an end, and things came to a head not long after that. I'm just glad he has sorted his life out. He's done a remarkable job to turn it all around.

When he got himself back together, he phoned me, but he had no need to apologise. At the end of the day, he's not a daft boy. He realised that I'd put him on a very good salary and that he hadn't done nearly enough to pay it back. I appreciated his call, but I knew it wasn't the real Andy McLaren I worked with at Reading. Deep down, he is a good guy, but other things were in control of his life at that time. I just wish I'd had the opportunity to work with him when he had no baggage.

Alan Pardew took over from Tommy. A lot of managers come in and gut the dressing-room as quickly as they can, especially when results haven't gone well. But Pardew spoke to me within his first couple of days in the job. He was genuine and honest and said, 'Andy, I like having wide men in my team. If you show the right attitude, I'll give you a chance to make it happen at this club.' It was the kind of pep talk most players want to hear – the new manager telling you that he sees you in his plans. But I wasn't in the right frame of mind to take in what he was saying. I was only interested in drinking. I couldn't stop.

Despite the new regime at the Madejski, I continued to turn up for training hung-over. John Gorman was Pardew's assistant, and he'd had enough of me. He quickly sussed out my problem and reckoned I was a waste of space. He was right. I couldn't defend myself against any allegation of that nature.

Being an alcoholic leads to the illness taking stuff from you, and there's no doubt drink took away my football career. I should have won more caps for Scotland; I should have played for a top club. I have no doubt I had the ability. During my time at United, Neil McCann was across the road playing for Dundee in the First Division. Neil is a year younger than me and was getting good press when he was about 20 years old. He won a move to Hearts in the summer of 1996 then got other big transfers to Rangers and Southampton for a combined total of about £3 million in fees. He also played 25 times for Scotland. Good luck to him. He worked hard to achieve good things in his career, but, with respect, I had more natural ability. I wasted my talent.

Gorman was really fed up with me, and I knew it was time to move on. Livingston offered to take me on loan, and I thought that getting back up the road would be the best thing for all involved. In mid-October, I signed a three-month loan deal at Almondvale. The club were in the First Division at that time and were managed by Ray Stewart.

In hindsight, I shouldn't have gone to Livi. I cheated them. The only reason I joined was because I knew I'd be in Scotland for Christmas with Claire, Dylan and Tyler and that there'd be a few good nights out over the festive period. As soon as Livi and Reading struck a deal for me, Ray was on the phone telling me to report in for training the following morning. I can't remember for sure, but I think he phoned me on the Tuesday asking me to train the next day. However, all I could think about was one more day of drinking. I knew I didn't need to go for training with Reading, which was a licence to have a 24-hour bender. I told Ray I couldn't get a flight and that I'd only be able to make it up the road two days later. Ray was having none of it and offered to book me a flight. He said, 'Andy, there's a flight every hour out of London. Hurry up and get here.' I don't think I made it in time for him. To be honest, my time at Livi is a bit of a blur.

When I was at Reading, I reckon I only took cocaine twice. I sourced it through a contact that knew a supplier in London, and he sorted me out. But I wasn't really that bothered about drugs at that stage. It was mainly Budweiser that I was interested in. That changed when I went to Livi. I was back living in Glasgow and was hitting the cocaine on a regular basis. I was wasting hundreds of pounds a week on cocaine and drink. It was all that mattered to me. I ended up totally skint. I also broke a rule I valued as a footballer: never to drink the night before a game. Throughout my career, I stuck to that. At times, I'd be choking for a drink on a Friday night, but I always managed to resist, although I often had a drink on a Thursday night. However, I convinced myself that it was acceptable to drink one Friday because the team had been announced after training the day before the game and I was on the bench. That, in my mind, meant I could do whatever I wanted. I was also pissed off that I wasn't starting for Livingston, as I felt I was good enough.

By late 1999, I was rattling every morning when I got out of bed. I couldn't go a full day without a few beers. I knew I was a mess, but it still wasn't enough to make me do something about it. I took the socialising too far when I was on loan from Reading. Most mornings, I would get a lift to training from Brian McPhee. I'd be steaming almost every time I stumbled into his car. He would literally have to carry me out of the car for training, because I'd be in such a deep sleep after getting practically no shut-eye the night before. Once I changed into my training gear, I'd try to grab 20 minutes' kip on a bench in the dressing-room before we headed out for our session.

Ray would often pick the team on a Friday, and when I was on the bench it was a signal for me to sink some Bud and snort some cocaine that night. I'd be in a helluva state on the day of the match and in no way ready to play a game of football at that level.

I really don't have many memories from my time at Livi. That period of my life is so hazy. I was constantly full of drink and drugs and had no time for football. Off the top of my head, I wouldn't have been able to tell you how many games I played for them or if I even scored a goal. I needed to check the history books to be sure, and according to the stats I made five starts and four appearances from the bench.

Ray Stewart: Andy's attitude was questionable right from the start. He was lazy in training and seemed to be there in person but not in mind and body. He'd have been as well being in the pub or in his bed for all the good he was doing in training.

His heavy drinking quickly came to light, and the boys in the dressing-room became aware of it. There was one game in which he was a sub, and I asked him to get ready to go on. I thought he looked like he'd had a right good session the night before, and he forgot to put his jersey on. He had to go back to the dressing-room to get it. In front of the whole crowd and the directors, he tried to kick open the metal gate to get access to the tunnel. But the gate opened out towards the pitch, and it rebounded into him. It didn't look too good.

After a few weeks, I was suspicious that there was more to it than just a few beers. Andy's eyes seemed to be sunk into the back of his head, so I asked a former policeman friend who had experience of dealing with such things to come to training for a couple of days to observe him.

My friend told me that Andy was 'spinning' and was definitely on something. I didn't want that kind of thing on my hands. I chose to keep it quiet and not go public. But I knew I had to sort it out or else the Livingston board would be on my case for not doing my homework properly. I spoke to Andy and told him that I wasn't having it but would protect him by not saying anything in public. We agreed that I should contact Reading and ask for them to take him back earlier than in the terms of the loan agreement. Reading were reluctant but eventually took him. If they hadn't taken him, I wasn't going to play him, and

I would have had to have gone public about my reasons why.

However, when the deal was clinched to sign him I was excited. Andy had talent, and I thought he'd help us win games. I just had no idea of the baggage he was carrying from his personal life. I'm glad he is living a better life now and has been dealing with his problems.

It became clear I wasn't covering up my unprofessional behaviour. Within a few days, Livingston knew I had a problem. I met Dominic Keane at a golf day a few years later. Dominic was chairman and part-owner of Livi. I told him that nobody could have helped me back then until I was ready to help myself.

Dominic Keane: When Ray approached me about signing Andy, I was keen. I knew he was a west of Scotland lad, and I knew he could be a bit wild in his social life, but I didn't quite realise the extent it had reached by the time he came to us. However, I looked upon Livingston as a family club and didn't want us to turn our back on a player without giving him a chance.

One thing I remembered about Andy from his days at Dundee United was that he always wore his shirt outside his shorts. I hated that. I told him that he had to keep his shirt tucked in at all times. I also told Ray Stewart and our kitman Danny Cunningham to make sure Andy adhered to my request. I was reminded that David Fernández and David Bingham were allowed to wear their shirts out. 'Aye, but they're the chairman's pets,' I said. 'They can do what they like!'

Within two minutes of his debut, a home game against Ayr United, his shirt was outside his shorts. I was furious. I calmed down when he jinked past a defender and sent over a cross for David Bingham to head home a few minutes later. He then switched wings and set up another goal for Bingham. We won 4–1. For every goal that went in, the players ran towards the directors' box and, to a man, all celebrated by taking their shirts out of their shorts. Brilliant.

It quickly turned sour after that. One morning before training – it was either a Thursday or a Friday – I could smell stale alcohol on Andy's breath. I wasn't happy. I told Jim Leishman [general manager] to have a word with him. Leish told me that he spoke to him and Andy gave him an assurance it wouldn't happen again – it was just a one off.

Things got worse, and Ray and Andy came to an agreement that he should go back to Reading. It was a shame because so many respected people in the game told me that Andy had the talent to go to the very top. I suppose, like many footballers before him, his is a sad tale of yet another Scotsman who failed to fulfil his potential. Unfortunately, football clubs can't watch every player in their squad 24 hours a day. As chairman, I would have liked to – to protect my investment and to give the club the best possible chance of winning every week – but it just couldn't be done.

In the past, when I was at United, I could drink all day and get away with it. I would often go out on a Thursday night, and on one occasion Tommy McLean caught me on the Friday morning stinking of booze. He told me I was being fined, but the amount I was going to have deducted depended on how well I played the next day in a Scottish Cup game against Motherwell. He would have been perfectly entitled to leave me in the stand for that game, but he knew he needed me. He also knew I could make a difference and, crucially, that I couldn't afford to be out of pocket. His judgement was spot on, as we won 4–1 and I scored two of our goals. I also won the Man of the Match award. In the dressing-room after the game, we looked at each other and there was a wee smile between us. He only fined me £50. That was one of my luckier moments. But I didn't always manage to come through the other side unscathed.

Livi knew they were wasting their time with me. My loan deal came to an end a few weeks ahead of schedule, and I went back to Reading. I didn't want to go, but I had no choice. And my first day back turned out to be a major turning point in my life.

8

TESTING TIMES

I WAS scheduled to be back at Reading on a Monday morning, but I had a good weekend partying and missed the flight back south. I flew down the next day and reported for training, but the training ground was pretty much deserted, as the first team had a game that night. I was delighted and my first thought was, 'Great. I can do a wee run then get out of here.'

Only five of us trained that day. We were standing in a group doing a few easy stretching exercises. I was out of the picture at the time and knew I would struggle to get back in the team. It was a dull and pretty damp morning, and as I looked up I noticed three men dressed in normal working clothes making their way across the training field towards us. I asked one of the boys who they were and was told that they were FA drug testers. My insides collapsed. I immediately thought back to the weekend just gone and remembered that I'd been drinking pretty much 24/7 and had taken cocaine and smoked cannabis at a house party in Glasgow.

I can recall that party well. I sat in the corner of the living room, freezing cold. Everyone was laughing and joking, but I felt lonely. I was no fun to be with, and I felt empty and dead inside. The way I was treating my family was not sitting easily with me, and I was feeling guilty.

The men from the FA approached us, and I tried my best to put them off, making out that the five of us were no-mark players and it would be a waste of time trying to test us. I told them they'd be better off coming back later in the week when the 'big boys' were around. But the men in suits weren't for making a-wasted journey and told us that we would all be tested after training.

I panicked and my initial reaction was to do a runner. I even thought about collapsing on the pitch and getting the boys to call an ambulance. I knew I had at least an hour to come up with some excuse. At that stage in my life, I had started 'speaking' to my old man. He'd been gone nearly a decade, but I took comfort from 'talking' things through with him. With the life-changing prospect of a drugs test on my mind and all the problems that could cause, I started to jog on my own, doing a few laps of the pitch. I knew my career was on the line in the next 60 minutes, and I was panicking. I looked up to the sky and felt my old man's spirit gazing down on me. I said, 'Dad, I need your help. You'll need to get me out of this one. Please, Dad. For fuck's sake, please.'

A small room inside our training ground complex had been set aside for the test. I was nervous, and right up until the last minute I contemplated doing a runner and dealing with the consequences later. 'Surely nothing can be worse than testing positive,' I thought.

I don't know what it was – perhaps it was my old man's guidance from above – but I plucked up the courage to go through with it. Standing outside the door with my heart pumping like never before, I took a deep breath and entered the room. This was it: the moment of truth. I was asked to urinate into a bottle and blow into a bag. I wasn't drunk at that point but thought I might still have some alcohol in my system. I had last drunk booze the night before.

Amazingly, I passed the alcohol test. However, the colour of my urine was close to a shade of green. The FA investigators gave me a sheet to fill in with all my details. There was also a section on the form that asked me to list any prescriptions or other medications I was taking. Knowing I had up to six grams of cocaine inside my system, and God knows what else, I thought it might get me off the hook if I told them I'd taken two Anadin painkillers the previous night for a headache. It was never going to work, but I thought it was worth a try.

Naively, I reckoned two painkillers would explain why I had tested positive and they'd take that as a legitimate explanation. Silly, I know, but I was thinking on my feet and trying anything to cover my tracks.

I was worried sick about the test and couldn't sleep or concentrate on football. I knew I had a couple of weeks before the club and I were informed of the results, and I thought it would be better to get away and come back to Scotland. The Reading captain Phil Parkinson had been going around telling people that the club were looking to slash the wage bill and pay a few players off. That sounded exactly what I wanted, so I approached Alan Pardew. I told him that I was homesick and couldn't settle. I wasn't enjoying my football and Reading were better off with me off the wage bill and getting a few quid for me from a transfer fee.

Pardew agreed to my request and said he'd speak to the board and make me an offer for an early departure. There was two and a half years of my contract remaining, and I worked out that I was due around £200,000 from wages and other built-in incentives, but I settled for something in the region of £32,000. The first £30,000 was tax free, so I was delighted. I could have got more than that if I'd haggled or got my agent involved, but I didn't want it getting too messy. I was handed a cheque and moved on with their best wishes. With a 32-grand cheque in my back hipper, I felt like I'd won the lottery and couldn't get to the bank quickly enough to cash it in.

I was also desperate to cash the cheque quickly because the club had no idea that they were about to receive the bombshell news that I'd tested positive in an FA drugs test. But at that stage of my life, I didn't have a conscience. I was totally selfish. I got a flight back to Glasgow and waited for my fate to be decided.

A few weeks later, a letter with an FA postmark arrived through the post. This was it. My result was in. I was shitting myself and put the letter on top of the fridge while I tried to compose myself. The letter sat there for an hour, then a couple of hours. Then another few hours.

I just couldn't open it. Whenever I walked into the kitchen, I stared up at the top of the fridge and felt my stomach churning. Stupidly, I reckoned all my problems would disappear if I didn't open it. For four days, I kidded on the letter didn't exist. Once I opened it, I was inevitably informed that I had tested positive for cocaine and cannabis abuse and was being called down to Leeds by the FA for a hearing.

The journey down to Yorkshire was hell. I was choking for a drink – it was the only way that I thought I could deal with it. Every ten minutes, the trolley laden with bevvy would rattle past my seat, but it wasn't rattling half as much as I was inside. I kept telling myself to have a Bud: 'Just one. It'll help your nerves.' Thankfully, I knew myself too well and realised I couldn't just have a curer. One drink would have led to a dozen drinks.

At the hearing, after telling me my results were positive, the FA informed me that they were immediately releasing a statement to the press. I asked them to delay it for ten minutes to allow me to phone Claire and members of my family. At that point, I wasn't bothered about myself. I was only concerned about how Claire and my mum would react. But within minutes of walking out of the Leeds Hilton Hotel, my phone was red hot and the news was out. The media all wanted to hear my version of events. The story was already all over the place, and I didn't get the chance to phone the people I wanted to so that they could hear it from me first.

I had no idea how big a story it was. It was headline news that night and made the front pages of the newspapers the following morning. Because of the coverage of the drug test, I was a nervous wreck throughout that whole sorry chapter. I couldn't handle the fact I was in demand for the wrong reasons.

On the day of the hearing, the juice on my mobile was running out, and I had to make a couple of calls before it died on me. But before any conversations were able to take place, I needed to calm myself. And the only way I knew how to properly calm myself was with a bottle of beer in my hand. I bought 12 Buds for the train journey back to Glasgow. I was the biggest story in Britain that day and had been found guilty of taking cocaine and cannabis, but the only way I knew how to deal with the fallout was to down a dozen beers.

I boarded the train in Leeds, downed a few beers and immediately felt a bit better. I then phoned my brother John and asked him to meet me at Glasgow's Queen Street Station. I also asked him to bring me a hat and scarf to help cover me up. God, you'd have thought I was on the run from prison.

When John picked me up, we ran to his car, and I locked the door as soon as I was in the passenger seat. I felt safe. Nobody could get to me. I could breathe again. John played with Glenafton Juniors at that time, and they had a light training session that night at Parklands Health and Fitness club on the south side of Glasgow. I went with him. Alan Rough was Glenafton manager, and I had a couple of pints with him after their training session. Roughy's company was exactly what I needed at that moment. He had a great sense of humour, which seemed to relax me a little. I wasn't in the mood for heavy conversation or somebody telling me where I had gone wrong. The truth could wait.

There was a lot of rubbish written about me for days after my test results were made public – stuff that was nowhere near accurate. For example, there was a piece on the front page of a newspaper about how my dad had died. That was sore to take, especially as my youngest brother was unaware of the circumstances. Because he was only a wee boy at the time, we had protected him.

It got to the stage that I stopped reading the papers because of the shite that was written about me. It wasn't that it bothered me too much; it was about what it was doing to Claire, our sons, my mum and granny. They were going to the shops and things were being said behind their backs. They didn't deserve that. Reporters sniffed about my house for days and chapped my mum's door. They also visited the local boozers in Castlemilk in an attempt to dig up some dirt on me.

Things settled down after a few days, but soon the circus was back in town when I had to report to the FA hearing in London to find out my punishment. My day of destiny had arrived: Wednesday, 8 March 2000.

Paolo Di Canio was up in front of the disciplinary panel that day charged with giving the finger to Aston Villa fans when he was playing for West Ham. Paolo got himself into some bother in England, but what a fantastic talent he was. He was brilliant for Celtic and really helped light up the Scottish game, along with Paul Gascoigne and Brian Laudrup, during a three- or four-year period from the mid-1990s.

In the lead up to my FA hearing, I was nervous and feared the worst. I continued to bevvy, as it was the only way I knew how to handle the pressure. Alcohol was my only coping mechanism.

At the hearing, I admitted I had an alcohol problem, and Craig Brown sent a letter of support that vouched for my character. It was a great gesture from him.

The FA were sympathetic towards me. The panel knew that I needed help, and rather than completely condemn and shatter my fragile existence they offered me the best possible assistance to get my life back into some form of decent shape. They wanted to send me to the Priory to get treatment and asked if I was willing to commit. My life was a lie at that time – it had been for some time. This was my chance to try to put things back together and build myself up again.

My agent John Viola and PFA rep Brendan Batson were with me

that day. I didn't realise how much the whole sorry episode was affecting me, but it was drummed into me when I met John before the hearing. He hadn't seen me in a couple of months, but as soon as he clapped eyes on me he knew I needed help. He couldn't believe how much my appearance had deteriorated, and I think his first words to me when we met were, 'Fuck sake, Andy, you don't look too well.' He was right, and his words had a profound effect on me. Agents get a lot of stick from fans, managers and even players. But John was there for me at a time when I was struggling to cope with the pressure. He told me he'd help me in any way, whether it was financial or emotional. 'Is there a Priory in Glasgow?' I asked. There was. I was going to go there.

I went in before Di Canio and thought that would be an advantage, but despite giving me a sympathetic hearing the FA suspended me indefinitely from football. When I came out, the television cameras were still there: BBC; STV; Sky; the lot. As I emerged into the street and walked along the road for a taxi, the photographers were right in my face. Click, click, click, click. I hated that. One of them ran backwards, lost his balance and crashed into a lamp post. I started to laugh. 'Well deserved,' I thought.

We stayed at a hotel in London that night. Charlie Miller played for Watford at that time, and he came to see me. I really appreciated the gesture.

Charlie is a fellow Castlemilk boy. He has unbelievable ability – a natural born footballer – and is able to do anything with the ball at his feet. His vision to pick out teammates and take out opponents with a single pass is frightening. We played together at Dundee United during my second spell at Tannadice, and we became really friendly. Charlie lived in Broughty Ferry with his family. Sometimes after training, I'd be like a lost soul, and Charlie would have me round for dinner. I'd also stay the night.

He played for Rangers and then spent a few years in Norwegian football. He has often been accused of not achieving as much in the game as he should have. That may well be true – I reckon

Charlie had the ability to win 50 caps for Scotland. However, Charlie always had a smile on his face and made sure those around him were smiling too. He had a positive outlook on life, and I admired him for that. We're still in touch, and we'll always remain friends.

In the hotel after the hearing, I was desperate for a drink. I really wanted to sink a few Buds, but I managed to resist. I suppose having company until the early hours and then being mentally tired from everything that had gone on that day left me exhausted and ready for bed.

The next day was Thursday, and on my return to Glasgow I was desperate to drown my sorrows the only way I knew how – in the comfort of my good friend Mr Bud. Just over 24 hours after admitting to an FA disciplinary hearing that I had a drink problem and was willing to sort myself out I was hammered.

Despite being drunk, I remember reading what the FA had to say about me in Thursday's paper:

> The player has admitted he has an alcohol problem. He has been ordered to return to us once he has been assessed and pending rehabilitation. We will then decide when he is fit to return to the game.
>
> It's clear the player has serious problems, and in the long term we want to help him. He wants to get back into the game, and if we can help him do that and overcome his problems we will.

I entered the Priory and had no idea what I was letting myself in for. I thought that I'd only need treatment for three months or so then I'd be brand new again. It never crossed my mind at that point that I'd be giving up alcohol for good. I had a friend's wedding to attend in the summer, and I thought I'd be ready to have a few drinks by then. I was kidding myself about that. One drink would have led to another. And another.

I didn't know it at the time, but getting into the Priory was one of the best things that ever happened to me. They had the right people there to help me on my road to sobriety. It was just a case

Purple bow ties and tartan troosers were all the rage when I was two! I'm looking a wee bit apprehensive in my fantastic clobber with granny Betty, who's holding baby John. (Courtesy of the author.)

The fantastic four . . . I'm left holding baby Jamie as Denise and John look on. (Courtesy of the author.)

One of the few pictures of the family together. I'm at the back with Dad and Mum, and John, Denise and Jamie are at the front. (Courtesy of the author.)

Not many Scots can say they've represented their country at a World Cup final, but there I am (front row, fourth from left) preparing to face Saudi Arabia at Hampden in June 1989. (Image courtesy of SNS Group.)

Gary Bollan and I join Ivan Golac's celebrations at the final whistle after we beat Rangers to lift the cup in 1994.

Party time as the Dundee United squad celebrate our cup final win at Hampden in 1994.

I'm doing cartwheels as I score against Aberdeen for Dundee United in November 1996.

Bert Konterman sends me tumbling in the penalty box as Killie faced Rangers in August 2000.

Alan Mahood is first to congratulate me after I scored
against Celtic at Parkhead in August 2000.

I finished off an incredible month by being awarded the
August 2000 Player of the Month award.
(Image courtesy of SNS Group.)

Gus MacPherson didn't score too many in his career – that's why Ally McCoist and I are so happy with his winner against Dunfermline in April 2001.

Flying the flag for Scotland as we head to Poland in 2001. Left to right: Kenny Miller, John O'Neil, Gavin Rae, Charlie Miller, Barry Nicholson, Stevie Crawford and yours truly.

I capped off a great season at Killie with a dream debut for Scotland as we faced Poland. (Image courtesy of SNS Group.)

Claire and I had an unforgettable holiday with the kids as we spent some quality time together in Florida in 2001. (Courtesy of the author.)

It Disney get better than this as Dylan and Tyler enjoy
a fantastic time in Florida. (Courtesy of the author.)

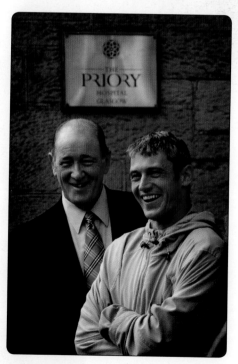

Outside the Priory with Ken Stewart – a pivotal time in my life.
(Courtesy of the author.)

The City of Discovery Cup in July 2006 may only have been a friendly, but I finally got closure with the Dundee United fans, who chanted my name that day. (Image courtesy of SNS Group.)

Nothing beats spending quality time with the family. Here I am this year with Claire and Tyler. (© Victoria Stewart/*Sunday Mail*.)

of when I was ready to open up and be honest. After a couple of days, I eventually did start to discuss things and felt the benefit of talking things through with people who knew exactly where I was coming from.

I can't speak highly enough of the Priory and its sensitive, caring and intelligent staff. But there's one person more than any other whom I have to thank for getting me there: my dad. I didn't appreciate it at the time, but, looking back now, he *did* get me out of my drinking habit, just like I'd asked him to as I jogged around the pitch on the morning of the FA drug test. In my mind, I have no doubt that if I hadn't been 'caught', I'd be dead by now. I was twenty-five at the time, and I reckon I had a maximum of one more season left in the professional game if I'd continued in the same direction. Beyond that, I think it's safe to say I'd have ended up with no money, no career inside or outside the game and mentally fucked. My dad died when he was 33, and I'm pretty sure I'd have gone before that age.

Several reasons make me say that. My tolerance to alcohol was reducing all the time, and I found myself struggling to cope after three or four beers. In my prime, I could drink a crate of Bud without batting an eyelid. Now, the shutters were coming down on me pretty quickly, and I wasn't comfortable with that.

In my final season at United, I suffered a few blackouts. The worst one was when I drove to Glasgow and was unable to recollect the journey. Normally, I'd remember everything about the night before, but during that period I wasn't too clever at recollecting stuff, and I'd go into the training ground in the morning and fish about for information about my behaviour from the boys.

If only I could have stuck to having three or four beers, like any normal person. But I could never understand how people were able to call it quits. To me, drinking was about getting drunk. That was my attitude from about the age of 13. I didn't even particularly like the taste. I used to smile when I heard some guys say, 'I could murder a nice, cold lager shandy to quench my thirst.' Eh? If I have a thirst on a hot day, I'd rather have a can of Irn-Bru. I was never, ever a social drinker. I just drank to get drunk and took alcohol for the effect.

However, I wasn't too bad a drunk. I was never aggressive or looked to cause trouble and pick a fight. Sure, Claire would tell you I was a pain in the arse with a drink down me: that I'd never shut up, blabbing away at 100 miles per hour. But I was cool with that. Perhaps if I'd been fighting and getting into trouble with the police, it would have made me stop sooner. Who knows?

When I left the Priory, I went to an FA hearing in Bradford at the start of May to prove I was clean and no longer dependent on alcohol. John Viola's business associate Michael Oliver accompanied me, and after answering a few questions about my lifestyle I proved to the panel I was fit and ready to make my return to the game. One of the panellists told me he was delighted with my progress. He told me he had genuine fears that I would never recover from the state I had been in a few months earlier. I was glad I'd proved him wrong.

The Priory saved my career. I went there for a reason: to try to get myself better; to stop living a lie; and, not to be too dramatic about it, to save my life and stand up and be counted as a partner, father and human being.

9

THE PRIORY

I **RECEIVED** a call on my mobile on the Friday morning. It was the Priory clinic to tell me that they had a place ready for me to come in the following morning to begin my 28-day rehabilitation programme. But I just wasn't ready to go. I told them that I wanted help, but it was too soon to tackle my demons head on. I tried to stall them, because, to be honest, I wanted a few more sessions on the drink.

I'd had a right good session the night before. I'd started boozing as soon as I'd arrived back from the FA hearing in London, enjoying a good few Buds in the house. So, I was slightly hung-over when I received the call from the Priory.

I made a decent attempt at fighting my corner and tried my best to fob them off, but they were having none of it and insisted on my attendance. They must have had to deal with hundreds of chancers like me – guys desperate to avoid the inevitable, desperate for another drink, desperate to avoid reality.

Two hours after the call, I was out shopping for some new clothes. I bought myself a tracksuit, underwear and flip-flops. I was told the Priory was a luxury establishment and the facilities included a gym.

That night, I was absolutely gagging for a drink. I was rattling. Sweating. I went to bed sober but couldn't sleep. Normally, I would just have got wired in, but I thought that if I stayed off the drink that night, the Priory would think I was fine. Naively, I reckoned they would think, 'This guy's not hung-over. This guy doesn't smell of alcohol. Let him go and we'll assign his bed to a more needy patient.' Stupid, I know.

My mate Geoff Brown picked me up and took me to the clinic. It was no more than a ten-minute drive from Castlemilk to another area on the south side, the more upmarket Mansionhouse Road, near Shawlands. Geoff dropped me off.

As I walked through the front door, it was just me and my sports bag. The years of boozing, damaging my body and my career, and neglecting my family had ended up leading me to a mental institution.

The irony wasn't lost on me as I stood there – it was a Saturday and I should have been preparing for a game. I was scared. This was real, and I had no place to hide.

I approached the reception area and was handed forms to fill in. What grabbed my attention most was the amount treatment cost. I'm sure it was in excess of £10,000. Without hesitation, I told them that I could not afford to pay, but they said that the English PFA were picking up the tab.

I wasn't sure of the restrictions at the Priory and thought that they might have taken my mobile phone. But I was allowed to hang onto it and was free to make contact with the 'outside world' whenever I wanted. I was also allowed to leave at any time. The front door was always open, but my freedom of movement was restricted during the first week, as they insisted I stay inside the building at all times for my own good. After that, I could go out to the shops or go for a walk whenever it suited me.

A lovely guy by the name of Ken Stewart was to be my main point of contact. He shook my hand at our first meeting and was straight to the point: 'Andy, did you have a drink last night?'

'No.'

'Well, you should have. You're in here for 28 days to dry out. It's going to be the biggest battle of your life, but we're here to help.'

I discovered Ken was a recovering alcoholic and obviously knew exactly what he was talking about. He gave me a big book on the AA and four or five books on alcoholism and told me to read them. I was taken to my room, and my first impressions were positive. My home for the next 28 days had a telly and en-suite facilities. It was like I had booked into a hotel. I wasn't in the mood for eating, but the nurse brought me some soup and sandwiches and that made me settle down a little bit.

I then had a one-to-one session with Ken, and he asked me if I had a drink problem. I told him I did but didn't have a real problem with drugs – I only took them when I was drunk. He'd been through it and knew the score. He told me it was going to be one day at a time. Battling alcoholism was about getting up in the morning and trying your best to get to bed the same night without touching a drop. There was no long-term strategy or planning.

I was naive about AA. I was learning about it all the time and picking up little things, but I still had a long way to go. During my first couple of days in the Priory, my goal was to get off the booze for two or three months to clean myself up, get my head back together and hopefully get a contract at a club to kick-start my career. A couple of months on the wagon then I'd get back on in style at my mate Richie's wedding to Sharon. I wanted to be back with a bang for their big day. Go to a wedding and not get blootered? No chance. There was no way I wanted to stop drinking for ever. I knew the Priory's plan was to take it one day at a time, but if Ken had informed me that their strategy was to get me off the bevvy for life, that would have fried my head. I was not ready to make that kind of commitment.

My first two days were very quiet, and there was little activity. The weekend was very relaxed, and patients who had been there more than a week, or ones who were back in for treatment, could go home. So there wasn't a lot planned on a Saturday and Sunday. In many ways, that was good for me. It gave me the chance to sleep and rest. I needed that, because it had been a traumatic few weeks, what with testing positive in the drugs test and all the negative publicity that had followed. I was also on medication for the first couple of days to help flush the alcohol out of my system.

But it wasn't easy. For the first three nights, I was still rattling – still sweating and feeling sorry for myself, trying to justify my drinking and all the times I was out of order. I was trying to come off the booze, but there was another side of me putting up one helluva fight, trying to justify my drinking. In the past, the bad side had won 99 times out of 100, but I couldn't allow it to kid me on any longer.

I also had suicidal thoughts in the Priory, although not to the extent of those I had when I was on the motorway on the way back from Edinburgh in 2006. When I was unable to sleep, the worst possible scenarios would go through my head, and I thought that I wasn't going to be able to win the battle. I used to ask myself if I would be better off dead than back on the drink.

On the Monday, we had a group session, and I found the whole scenario totally embarrassing. About seven or eight people were in the group, and they came from all walks of life: teachers, lawyers, doctors and professionals with a few quid to spend to get their lives back on track. The Priory also treats people with eating disorders, stress, depression and other things. I was on the addiction programme.

There was one other guy in the group by the name of John. The rest were women. I was surprised at that. They were all comfortable speaking about their problems, but I wasn't ready to open up. I was the new guy on the block, and I eased myself in gently.

I've never found talking to be a problem, but there was more of a need to write things down in the Priory. We had to keep a daily diary, but, to be honest, I really couldn't be bothered. I was never one for having a pen in my hand. It seemed to come naturally to the rest of them, however. Starving my body of drink was hurting me – I was being sick and I was rattling – and I didn't think that they would want to hear me reading that out. And I was just as reluctant to speak about it. The truth was that without a drink inside me I felt stripped of self-confidence and self-worth and was full of doubts. I was worried that I'd say the wrong thing and the others would laugh at me, labelling me a stupid footballer.

They all spoke about how they were having wonderful days. I thought, 'Fuck me, I must really be in a bad way.' So to try to make myself look good and keep up with the rest of the group, I started to make up things to put in my diary. I thought that telling lies was the only way I was going to get out of the loony bin.

To be honest, I hated my first two weeks in the clinic. The only pleasure came during the second week when I was allowed to go home to see Claire and the boys and go for a run in Queen's Park to improve my fitness in the hope of getting a club when I came out.

I do remember one thing that helped my rehabilitation in the Priory. I had a policy of not looking at the papers, because I was sick of reading negative stuff about me, but there was one article that gave me encouragement and offered me hope. A reporter had managed to get a hold of George Best, who offered me comforting words of advice. George knew better than most what it was like to be a major boozer, but he told me to keep battling my addiction and to try to remain positive. His good wishes meant so much to me. He'd never met me and wouldn't have known me from the next guy in the street, but he took time out to say a few words. I think he was also in hospital at that time. There's no doubt that gave me a lift. It was a real boost and helped lift the depression I was suffering from during the early days.

The real breakthrough came on 14 March, which was, ironically, the anniversary of my dad's death. That was the day I attended my first AA meeting and is the day I look upon as being my first of sobriety in the new chapter of my life. There was a boy at the meeting called Barry, and I clicked with him straightaway. He was a recovering alcoholic and spoke my language. I could identify with him and felt relaxed in his company.

At my first few meetings, I wore a skip cap pulled down over my eyes to hide my identity. I didn't speak much, preferring just to listen and watch what was going on. I wasn't giving anything away, but I felt progress was being made after that initial meeting. I started to realise what the Priory was all about and exactly why I was there. I had to do that before I was going to get anywhere. For the first two weeks, I just looked upon my stay at the clinic as a visit to some glorified health farm. The truth was, though, I was in a psychiatric hospital, albeit with a fancy name and reputation, and I was there to try to restore my sanity.

After my initial sickness and shaking, my body was starting to get used to not drinking, and after the first two weeks I became comfortable. Too comfortable. I felt safe and was even trying to help newcomers settle in. I was no longer the new start but an experienced hand. Well, in my book, anyway! But there was also a fear of going back out into the big, bad world. I knew I couldn't get a drink in the Priory, but as soon as my 28 days were up there would be temptations every minute of every day. At the pictures with the kids? Drink available. Shopping for bread and milk? Bud somewhere on the shelves.

It was for this reason that I asked the Priory to allow me out to go to a restaurant for a bite to eat with Claire. They couldn't have stopped me from going, but I thought it was best to ask and give them their place. And I could understand their reservations about allowing me to go to a place with booze on tap – it wasn't as if I had my shorts and trainers on and was going for a run.

We went to Di Maggio's, just a five-minute walk from the Priory. It must have been one of the very few times I had ever been totally sober with Claire on a social occasion. I'd normally be drunk, or just a couple of beers from topping up my intake from the night before, talking like there was no tomorrow and doing Claire's nut in, if truth be told. But on that occasion I struggled to speak and didn't know what to say to her. It was horrible. Claire was probably oblivious to my anxiety, but it was another sign of a breakthrough that I could go out and not have a drink. It was also just nice to sit down and breathe a huge sigh of relief. And it was good to have Claire there for me. I'd never really given a fuck about her and the boys, yet I wanted them to be there for me when I asked. And thankfully they were. Claire was also scared, but she was rock solid for me and never crumbled.

A couple of lads in the Priory called Bob and Tom were also a terrific help. Every Tuesday, there was a meeting for current and previous Priory patients – between 30 and 40 would attend. Bob and Tom had been in before and regularly attended the Tuesday meeting. They told me not to feel alone and that they would help me get through it. They said alcoholism was a war I couldn't fight on my own and that I would have to lean on friends and talk to people. Their words were nice and just what I needed to hear.

The daily routine became less of a chore, and I was starting to contribute. I was eating breakfast at 8 a.m. and looking forward to the 9.30 get-together. However, I found some of the language they used quite hard to understand. Of course, I now know it's 'AA speak', but at that time it was alien to me – things like 'There is a power greater than yourself to stop you drinking' and stuff about 'God giving you guidance'.

When I was able to concentrate, I'd often sit there and think, 'What are they talking about?' For a while, I thought they might be trying to ram God down my throat, and that just wasn't for me. I was brought up a Roman Catholic but had long since stopped practising my faith. I told them I didn't believe in God, and that was cynical of me. I hope I didn't offend any of them, but I was telling the truth, and it was an environment in which people were encouraged to be honest.

At the end of the meetings, I'd often go to John and ask him to simplify what the others were saying. John was good that way.

He never judged me and always wanted to help. He was great at explaining things.

On my good days, I'd look at people and think, 'If they can do it, so can I.' On other days, I would cause a bit of havoc. I started to confront other patients if I thought that they were talking bullshit. One woman said that she only drank a couple of glasses of wine here and there and had no idea why she was in the Priory. I told here that she was in denial and she should stop wasting her own time and ours. I just lost the plot and stormed out. I went home. I walked for about ten minutes and then jumped into a taxi. Claire couldn't believe it when I turned up on the doorstep. Ken phoned me and asked when I was coming back. I shouldn't have gone off on one at that woman, but Ken said it was a good thing that I showed emotion and a desire for her to be honest.

As I've said before, there are 12 steps in AA as part of the ongoing recovery programme, and the fourth one involves writing down your life story. I've heard a few over the years. People have been in tears reading them out, and I've been in tears listening to them. When I was in the Priory, I wrote my story and stripped myself bare. Well, as far as I felt I could – probably down to my underwear. It was emotional, and I was in tears writing my story. Yet I left bits out – aspects I wasn't ready to talk about, not to a group of strangers. People knew I was holding back, and I admitted that. I told someone about being abused, but I wasn't willing to write it down.

The AA is a wonderful organisation, but it is not a confessional box. You are encouraged to find someone you trust and call them your 'sponsor'. I find that a little bit too formal, so I call the people I trust and open up to my 'pals'. I have, and always will, talk to them about anything. In the past, I've regretted being so honest, but that was because I stupidly believed they would judge and laugh at me. Nothing could be further from the truth. They are all special people.

Towards the end of my 28 days in the Priory, I felt really good and really strong. I knew I was going to be able to give it a go and take their advice and help on board. Gone was the little voice inside my head telling me that after a few weeks the doctors would say to me, 'Well, Andy, you've done well recently, so treat yourself to a few pints, and we'll see you in a few months' time.' I had come to terms with the fact that at the start of every morning when I got out of bed the first thing I had to say to myself was, 'I'm not going to have a drink today.'

During my stay in the Priory, I attended eight or nine AA meetings, some on the premises, some in other parts of Glasgow. To be truthful, I thought I was too young to be in AA. The others looked about 50 or 60, and I reckoned they'd had a right good go at it. But I've learned so much from many of them.

At first, when I went to outside meetings, I tried to hide my identity and avoided attending any in Castlemilk. God, I'd been on the front pages of every newspaper in Scotland and made the headlines on the six o'clock news, yet I was worried someone from Castlemilk would recognise me at a meeting. That's how fucked my head was.

After getting that daft notion out of my head, I was taken aback to be recognised at a meeting by a woman who was well into her 70s. I was standing with a good friend of mine called Old Chris, and the woman was staring intently at me. 'It is you,' she said. 'It is you, isn't it? Come on, I know it is.'

So, Old Chris said to her, 'Well, who the hell is he?'

'You're Gary Lineker, aren't you? The boy from the crisps advert. Aye, you can't fool me, son.'

I had my baseball cap on, and she had clocked my grey hair peeking out from underneath. I was ready to tell her she'd got the wrong footballer, but Old Chris seized on the moment and said, 'Look, love, don't tell anyone. Keep it to yourself. He'll lose his job on the telly if anyone gets to hear about this.'

She grabbed hold of my arm and said, 'Don't worry, son. I won't tell a soul.' Things like that made me laugh. I definitely needed moments like that.

I left the Priory on a Saturday morning, 28 days after I'd signed in. It was an achievement to get through it, and I never even got to sleep in the 'Torture Chamber', which was a room in the Priory with a window that overlooked a pub across the road. People would sit out in the nice weather, sipping a cold beer, unaware of how jealous they might be making someone feel!

I was given an AA learning pack when I left the Priory. It was helpful and gave me some pointers on how to deal with alcohol. The members of my group also wrote some nice words of encouragement on a card that they presented to me on my day of departure. And Ken Stewart wrote a very positive report to the PFA about me. He told them I had made a real effort and was fully aware of the problems I had to tackle.

But I was still apprehensive about going out into the big, bad world. I'd been shielded from it for a wee while, and now temptation was all around me. Could I deal with it? The support I had from people inside the Priory and at AA, and also the cards and letters I received from the public, made me feel very special, and I did not want to let anyone down.

Billy McKinlay, my former teammate at Dundee United, also sent me a letter. Billy was a bit older than me and wasn't really in the 'gang' of young players at United, but he still looked out for us all. The man we called 'Badger' was a fantastic midfielder – he had great energy and commitment, and was good for a goal from the edge of the box. Badger could also be nasty on the pitch if it was required. He had an eye for a pass, and I knew if I made a run into a dangerous area, he would find me. He had a ferocious temper, and I remember he attacked me in the dressing-room after a game when I told him to fuck off. I was scared he was going to batter the living daylights out of me, and a few of the lads had to pull him away from me. I learned my lesson that day and made sure I never messed with Badger again.

His letter to me was touching and straight from the heart. It was full of nice words, and it cheered me up. He told me to battle against my illness and not to give up on football because I had too good a talent to waste. It really inspired me, and things such as that letter helped me to get my life and career back together.

However, my most enlightening times came from being in the company of Old Chris. He'd been there, seen it and done it. He didn't take any bull and would put me in my place if necessary. I spent a lot of time with him at AA meetings. I regarded him as my main pal. He didn't have a magic wand, but he could make me believe that he had the answers to my problems.

Stupidly, I believed being off the drink would mean that life would be perfect – the sun would shine every day, and the bills would stop coming through the door if I stayed sober. Of course, life is not like that. The only guarantee you get from AA is that if you don't touch a drink, you won't get drunk.

Joining the AA has been so rewarding for me, especially sharing stories and having so much in common with the person sitting next to me. One of the guys was a millionaire and lost his fortune when he was on the drink. He got back to having a right few quid in his pocket again but lost it all. Whether he had a million in the bank or not made no difference to him in terms of how happy he was. The only difference it made to him was how much he had in his pocket to spend on alcohol.

My experience in the Priory was beneficial. And I can't thank the English PFA enough. They stood by me and paid for me to receive the very best treatment to help me get my life back together. If I had been in another walk of life, it's highly unlikely an employer or my union would have paid in excess of £10,000 for me to receive their specialist care. Thanks for not abandoning me and thanks for believing in me.

I felt weird the day I walked out of the Priory. I had hardly been sober during the previous five years. And if I hadn't been drinking, then I'd been thinking about where my next drink was coming from. It was different now. The Andy McLaren that walked out of the Priory was totally different from the Andy McLaren that walked in.

I got a taxi back to the house, but it felt strange to be home. Claire and my mum were kind of walking on eggshells around me. I didn't want that.

I made it to Richie and Sharon's wedding. I arrived sober and left sober. I never did get those Buds I promised myself, but I still had a great night.

10

SIGNING FOR KILMARNOCK

I KNEW my lifestyle would have to change dramatically if I wanted to get myself back on the rails. My immediate priority was to stop drinking. It was difficult, of course, but by taking it one day at a time the days started to get easier the longer I stayed dry. As I began to get a grip on my situation, I started to think about getting a job again and earning some money the only way I knew how: playing football.

I was itching to get back, and at the end of May I attended the Scottish Football Writers' Association Player of the Year dinner, as I thought that would be a good way to mingle with football people again, press some flesh and get the word out that I was on the mend. It worked out really well. I spoke to a number of Premier League managers and dozens of players, and I felt great. I didn't feel alienated in any way, which had been my fear on my way to the dinner that night. Rob MacLean asked to interview me for BBC *Sportscene*, and we arranged a meeting for the following week. It was a positive step to do something for television.

Barry Ferguson was voted the Player of the Year that night and was obviously busy and in demand from well-wishers, fans and fellow players. But I'll always remember that he took time to come down from the top table to talk to me. It was his night, and we didn't really know each other too well, but his words of encouragement were genuine. I've nothing but respect for Barry.

The whole event gave me a massive lift, and I felt it gave me the impetus and the confidence to get back into the game. Now it was just a case of waiting for the phone to ring and finding out what John Viola had for me. I didn't expect anything to happen overnight, as it was the end of the season and people were preparing to go on holiday.

A few weeks later, I had four interesting offers from SPL clubs. One from Alex McLeish at Hibs, one from Sandy Clark at St Johnstone, Paul Sturrock wanted to take me back to Dundee United and Bobby Williamson made it clear that he wanted me to sign for Kilmarnock. It was a boost to have a number of clubs interested in me. I'd gone from four months earlier being banned from football by the English FA to getting my act together and being approached by four SPL clubs.

I travelled to Tannadice to meet Sturrock. I was nervous returning to the city where it all began for me as a teenager. It was the scene of so many of my crimes – my downfall, even. Sturrock was positive and was glad to see me getting my life back on track. We'd had our differences, and I didn't agree with some of his methods, but he was still a top coach and taught me so much about the game. In the afternoons, I just wanted to go to the pub and the bookies, but he insisted I come back for extra sessions. Paul's knowledge of the game is different class, and I enjoyed a good relationship with him.

There's no doubt that had I not been on the booze, Paul would have really improved my game, and I'm confident he could have helped me to win a move to a bigger club. But I also couldn't forget that when he came back to United as manager he sold me to Reading. In hindsight, that probably proved how astute a boss he was, because he knew I was on the slide and decided it was better to cash in on me. There are no hard feelings between us.

I was tempted to go back to Tannadice but didn't think it would be in my best interests to return to Dundee. I needed a clean break from there. When I emerged from Sturrock's office, wee Jim

McLean was waiting for me in the corridor. Never one for putting an arm around your shoulder or offering a bit of sympathy, wee Jim just ripped into me. 'You've been a disgrace, and it's time for you to grow up,' he said. I laughed at him, but it was more of a nervous laugh – it was not meant to be derogatory.

Sandy Clark arranged to see me at McDiarmid Park. The meeting was positive, and it was a boost for my ego to hear him say I would be a good addition to his team. He was persuasive, and the offer was tempting. Sandy seemed like a guy I would have enjoyed playing for. I didn't manage to meet Alex McLeish face to face, but he made a verbal offer to give me training facilities with a view to offering me a contract.

I met Bobby Williamson in John Viola's office in Glasgow city centre. We clicked right away. I'm from Castlemilk and Bobby hails from Easterhouse, both tough areas in Glasgow. A spade is a spade where Bobby comes from. He told me he wouldn't place unreasonable demands on me and offered me a three-month deal. He assured me that I could have a day off here and there to attend meetings and basically do whatever was necessary to battle my addiction, which would ultimately improve my game. Bobby wasn't interested in passing judgment on me for my past demeanours or the fact I was an alcoholic. I liked that.

When it became public knowledge that I had a drink problem, the only offer I received was from Berwick Rangers. Their chairman Jimmy Crease – a decent man with good intentions – offered me a chance at Shielfield, and I was grateful. But I knew that I was in no state to play football at that time, and the English FA had banned me, anyway. It scared me that part-time football might be my level in the future, which wasn't a pleasant thought when I had been a full-time player for more than a decade. I was also approaching what should have been the peak years of my career.

Therefore, it was fantastic to receive four offers of full-time football, and I weighed up my options carefully. I considered the good and bad points about Dundee United, St Johnstone, Hibs and Kilmarnock. It was Rugby Park that ticked almost all my boxes. Bobby had built a good team, and they had Ian Durrant and Ally McCoist on board, which was another positive. They had won the Scottish Cup in 1997 and had qualified regularly for European football. Geographically, Kilmarnock was only half an hour from my house, which meant I wouldn't need to move. Staying in Glasgow was vital, because I'd found a couple of AA meetings I was comfortable going to and people whom I trusted. I definitely didn't want to jeopardise any of that. I'd also enjoyed playing at Rugby Park whenever I'd been there with another club. The home support were passionate, and I believed Killie was on the up and up. I'd made my mind up. I informed the other managers I wouldn't be accepting their kind offers, and the day after meeting Bobby I told him I wanted to sign for Kilmarnock.

Bobby Williamson: I tried to sign Andy for Kilmarnock when I heard there was going to be a parting of the ways at Dundee United. But I was told by an agent that it was best for Andy to go down south and play.

What happened to him at Reading has been well documented, and it must have been a turbulent period in his life. But when I knew he was looking for an opportunity to get back into the game after he had been to the Priory and the English FA was satisfied he was ready to go back on the straight and narrow, I had to go for him.

He had offers from a few clubs, and I was as honest as I could be when I met him to discuss the possibility of joining Kilmarnock. I always knew the boy had talent – he was good with either foot, strong in the air and had pace. If his troubled past was well and truly behind him, I knew he'd be an asset for us. I was willing to give him the chance. I believe we all make mistakes in life and should all be allowed to redeem ourselves. I was delighted when Andy told me he'd be trying to kick-start his career with us.

My gut instinct about joining Killie was sound, and I enjoyed playing under Bobby. I knew his door was always open, and I could talk to him at any time about anything. That's what I needed at that stage of my life. His man management was brilliant, and that's why he had a happy dressing-room. He is a brilliant human being, and I have nothing but respect for him.

However, I was really nervous about meeting my new teammates on my first day at Rugby Park. I knew they'd be unsure as to what was acceptable to ask me about the drink and drugs and what was deemed to be overstepping the mark, and I hardly slept a wink the night before my first day. But I didn't need to be nervous. Ian Durrant made sure of that.

11

KEEPING IT CLEAN

I'D NOT been in a dressing-room for seven months, and I missed it. I missed the patter, the silly pranks and the endless wind-ups. I missed receiving a nice massage whenever I wanted and the long, hot baths at lunchtime. I missed the gossip that would filter its way into the dressing-room from other clubs. Most of all, I missed putting on my boots and scoring goals or setting them up every morning in training.

I didn't really know any of the Kilmarnock players very well, and I wondered how they would treat me. The last thing I wanted was for them to tip-toe around me because of what I'd been through. I wanted them all to act naturally around me. Time would tell.

I'd heard and read so many stories about Ally McCoist and Ian Durrant that I thought they might do something to break the ice when I first stepped into the dressing-room. Then I thought about taking the bull by the horns and walking in on my first day carrying a crate of Bud just to take the sting out of things. I thought better of that. No, it was best to let things happen naturally.

Arrangements had been made for me to meet Mark 'Mavis' Reilly, Ally Mitchell and Chris Innes at East Kilbride so that we could travel to training together. Usually, I'd be talking away at 100 miles an hour, but I was nervous and hardly said a word to the three of them as we made our way down the road.

When we arrived at the stadium, I walked into the home

dressing-room and found a peg to hang my clothes on. Within seconds, Durrant was on me, and he ripped me apart: 'Fuck sake. Is this the road this once-fine club is going down, eh? Signing guys like this. What chance have we got boys, eh?' The lads were laughing. It was exactly what I wanted. The ice was well and truly broken and nothing was now off limits.

From that moment, I knew that I would get on well with Durranty. We had a similar sense of humour, although he's better than me at destroying people with his put-downs! But he always does it with a smile on his face and with the intention of lighting the place up. There's never any malice.

The first training session was outdoors at the Magnum Centre in Irvine. I think Bobby Willamson might have asked Paul Sturrock what kind of trainer I was. In the past, I had never trailed behind, and, in fact, I usually led the way. Therefore, I still had a good reputation when I joined Kilmarnock, despite my previous drinking habits. We were put into groups for running exercises, and I was in the last one with the quicker lads. We were expected to overtake the boys in front of us, and most of the others did. But I struggled and was left behind. I suppose it was to be expected, as, apart from a few runs round Queen's Park when I was in the Priory, I hadn't really bothered about my fitness. I realised how much sharpness I'd lost in that six- or seven-month period, and I was shocked. To be fair, I was flying three or four days later. Normal service had been resumed.

After our run, the balls came out, and I was in my element. I was buzzing, and it was a brilliant feeling finally to have a ball at my feet again. After all the publicity, all the media attention and all the pain of those previous seven months, I was at last able to do what I knew I was best at – playing football. It had been too long – far too long.

We played a full-scale practice game, and I was on the right wing. Durranty was in my team, and he controlled the game. He'd create space for himself, receive the ball and then look for me. He gave me the ball all day long – simple but so effective. I was happy to get Durranty's constant supply of quality passes. I was flying past Garry 'Hooky' Hay and set up a goal for Gary Holt to bullet home a header from one of my crosses. I felt so good about myself. It had been a while since I'd got that kind of buzz from a game of football.

We went to a training camp in Austria for our final preparations for the new season. Our hotel was in the middle of nowhere. I was delighted, but some of the boys complained because there was nowhere for a night out. Normally, I'd have been the first guy to moan about the situation, but the peace and quiet meant one thing to me – no temptation.

The training sessions put on by Bobby and coaches Jim Clark and Gerry McCabe were good. The balance was right between ball work, set-plays and continuing to top up our stamina levels. Some of the lads had the energy to play tennis in the afternoons, but I was happy to rest. I also used my spare time to get myself mentally right for the up-and-coming campaign.

Pre-season trips can be boring, there is no doubt about that. You need to find good company, and I enjoyed spending time with Durranty. We all know what a fantastic footballer he was, but I also got to know him as a person, and he was very clever. I'm sure he was encouraged by Bobby to speak to the younger players and point them in the right direction. Durranty's man-management skills were terrific. We'd walk together to training, and he'd tell me I was doing well and looking good. He also made sure he asked simple but important questions like, 'How are you today?' That might sound daft, but it was such a big help. He'd had his own problems during his career – albeit with injury and not drink and drugs – and he knew what it was like to try to come back after being out for such a lengthy period. I was able to open up to him. He's a gem of guy. Hey, don't get me wrong – he also continued to destroy me with his one liners in front of the other boys.

Our first league game of the 2000–01 season was away to St Mirren. The week before the match, Durranty asked me to travel with him to the training pitch, a couple of miles away from Rugby Park. He told me I was in line to start at Love Street, and I was so happy. But the cocky side of me also came out, and I thought, 'So I fucking should be. I've been doing well.'

Another reason I was on such a high at that time was because I'd received a letter from Alan Pardew, my former gaffer at Reading. He wrote to wish me well at Kilmarnock and to say how pleased he was to see me back in the game. The letter mentioned he had watched a guy slowly take himself apart with alcohol, eventually all the way to the grave, and he had worried that the same thing was going to happen to me. It struck me that his letter came straight from the heart, and it meant a lot to me. It also hit home again that I'd really blown things at Reading and could not waste the opportunity I was being given at Kilmarnock. It was time to screw the nut and take responsibility for my actions. There was no one else to blame if this move didn't work out.

I've never thanked Pardew for that letter, but I was touched by it. He's a good guy, and I hope to meet him again one day and shake him by the hand to thank him. I've looked for his results ever since and was pleased to see him take West Ham to the Premiership in 2005 and all the way to that memorable FA Cup final at the Millennium Stadium in Cardiff a year later when they lost to Liverpool on a penalty shoot-out after a dramatic 3–3 draw.

I knew I was ready for the SPL when I played in a pre-season game against Clyde. I scored a goal and set one up. It felt great. My whole life was in good condition, and I was happy. I was going to AA meetings and feeling the benefits of staying sober.

Having breakfast was a big thing. I loved getting up in the morning, enjoying some fun with my sons as they got ready for school and then having some toast and cereal. Now, I'd never miss breakfast, but I didn't start eating the first meal of the day until I was 26!

Even getting up in the morning and putting on fresh gear felt great – it gave me a positive start to the day. In the past, I'd get in at four in the morning, grab a few hours' kip and then throw on the same clothes to go to training the next day. I'd be honking of booze and cigarettes. Awful.

And it turned out that Durranty was spot on: I was in the starting line-up for the game against St Mirren. I had a nightmare in the first half, and the Love Street fans gave me absolute pelters with their chants of 'junkie' and 'alky' every time I touched the ball. I was angry with myself at half-time. The spotlight was on me that day, and, in hindsight, I probably let everything get to me. I was wound up and desperate to impress. Probably too desperate. My performance suffered, and it wasn't helped by the abuse I was taking from the supporters. I knew I could do better, and at half-time I decided I had to start the second half flying. I wanted to get the last laugh on the home fans, and I wanted to play well for my family, Bobby and Kilmarnock.

After the break, Durranty started getting plenty of possession and just kept giving me the ball. I was in the mood, and I hit the crossbar with a shot. We then won a free-kick in a decent position. We had good presence inside the box, with the likes of Kevin McGowne and Gary Holt, so I sent the ball over to the back post, and Holt was there to charge in and head home past Ludovic Roy. The boys all celebrated the goal, and I expected them to come to me to congratulate me on my assist! Holt got all the plaudits instead! I had five or six people there that day, including my mum, who was in the St Mirren end. I waved to her after we scored.

After about 80 minutes, I told Bobby that I was knackered and had nothing left to give. I had cramp and wasn't able to put in the defensive shift that was required for the last ten minutes as the Saints tried to grab an equaliser. I was subbed, and we held on for a terrific result. It was a great start to the season, both for me and the club. I was also happy to have shut up the Saints fans after the verbal abuse they had given me throughout the game.

Winning the first league game of the season is so important. It gives you confidence and something to build on. Therefore, training was good in the build-up to our next game – at home to Rangers. After my contribution against the Saints, there was always going to be major attention on me, although the media never need an excuse when coverage of the Old Firm is required. Newspapers, television and radio all wanted to speak to me, and I was happy to talk about the game.

I was even happier twenty minutes into the match when we were two goals up and I'd scored both. Rangers had signed Bert Konterman and Fernando Ricksen that summer for big money but both had torrid starts to their Ibrox careers. From early on in the game, I knew that they were not at ease and were there for the taking. Within the first few minutes, I took possession and ran into the box. Konterman was hesitant as he prepared to tackle me, and he tripped me up as I knocked the ball past him. The referee Tom Brown gave us a penalty.

Christophe Cocard was nominated as the Kilmarnock penalty taker, but I had odds of 14–1 to score the first goal, and I'd told my friends and family to put a few quid on me, as I was confident of producing a good performance. I grabbed the ball as quickly as I could and didn't give Christophe a chance to stake a claim. I sent Stefan Klos the wrong way. One of my mates won £280 on that goal.

Jerome Vareille then sent me clean through, and I outpaced Lorenzo Amoruso and Konterman to get a strike in on Klos. He got a hand to the ball, but my shot was too powerful and it squeezed over the line. We were two up, and Rangers were in a state of shock. They were handed a lifeline when Kevin McGowne was harshly sent off. Down to ten men, we were always going to struggle. Billy Dodds scored two to even things up, and Kenny Miller and Tugay sealed a 4–2 victory for Dick Advocaat's team.

Despite the result, I was on a high. I had to be selfish at that stage of my career – it was all about me playing well to secure a longer contract. I got back to the house and was surprised that Claire and the boys were not there to greet me. After all, I was the returning hero. I had scored two against Rangers, so why no brass band? Why no red carpet? I was buzzing, and in the past I would have been straight out on the booze. Sitting in the house alone, every bit of me wanted to get drunk. For the first time in a while, I was finding it hard to control my urge for alcohol. I was choking for a few Buds and wanted to go to the pub.

My way out was to phone Old Chris. I'd only met him a few months before, but he pretty much knew me inside out. Or, to be more accurate, knew alcoholics inside out. I phoned, made some small talk and then we had a wee chat about the game. He then said, 'Right, enough bull. What's wrong with you?'

'I'm choking for a drink.'

'That's the way you should feel,' he told me. 'You're an alcoholic.'

'I know. It's just that I'm pissed off that Claire and the boys aren't here so I can tell them about the game.'

'Well, forget that and go and keep yourself busy. Get the Hoover out and do the dishes. That'll keep you busy for at least half an hour.'

Before I knew it, I'd vacuumed the house, and I was standing at the sink when Claire walked in. The look on her face when she clocked me washing the dishes was priceless. She must have thought I'd finally flipped. But thankfully Old Chris's advice worked. It was a great day all round – I scored two goals at Ibrox, didn't have a drink and the house was spotless!

We played Celtic the following weekend, and once again there was a lot of media attention on me. It was public knowledge that I was only on a three-month contract, and Bobby was already being asked by reporters if I would be offered an extended deal. His comments were all positive, and he made it clear that he wanted the Kilmarnock board to give me a lengthier deal. But, knowing I was available for free at the end of September, a few managers had taken note of my form and registered an interest with John Viola.

I was receiving some really positive publicity, and it was a welcome change after the rubbish that had been written about me earlier in the year. Martin O'Neill was sniffing about me for Celtic, and Wolves were also interested in taking me back down south.

Playing for Killie at Parkhead was the perfect platform to show what I was made of and continue my good work from the previous week. Again, I opened the scoring, and it was another belter. Alan Mahood passed to me, and I took on Stéphane Mahé and Tom Boyd. I charged towards Celtic's penalty area, and the goal just opened up. I let rip from about 20 yards, and the ball flew into the net past Jonathan Gould. I fell back as I struck the shot and ended up on my backside. The next thing I knew, all of the lads were on top of me.

Dylan was in the front stand, sitting with my old pal Jimmy. I looked for them after the goal, and I'll never forget the smile on Dylan's face. He looked so happy and proud of his dad. That meant so much to me. A few other people I knew were also happy, because I'd told them to back me for first goal again, and this time I was a 16–1 shot. Jimmy had a few quid on me and was also a Celtic supporter. His coupon came up, and his day ended perfectly, as O'Neill's side came back to win 2–1. Henrik Larsson levelled it after the break and then set up the winner for Tommy Johnson. Martin Baker was sent off near the end – another man dismissed against the big two under dubious circumstances. Once again, we had outplayed an Old Firm side for long spells but had nothing to show for it at full time. We almost made it 2–2, but Cocard headed just wide after I'd set him up with a cross.

One thing I'll never forget about that game was Tommy Johnson's kind words at the end. He came over, gave me a cuddle and told me he was delighted to see me doing so well after everything I'd been through. I didn't know Tommy and thought it was a lovely gesture. We became teammates at Kilmarnock two seasons later, and I reminded him about that day.

The downside about the Parkhead game was the chants from the home fans of alky and junkie. Chris Sutton, who also used Viola as his agent, got me two tickets for the 'posh' seats near the directors' box, which I gave to Claire and her aunt. A few Celtic fans in that area chanted abuse towards me during the game, and it was very uncomfortable for her. But being on the receiving end of verbal abuse from opposition fans became the norm during that time. And, indeed, it's something I've had to live with for most of my career since.

I've tried to not let it get to me, but it bothered me when I heard that my mates had been caught up in a fight during a game trying to defend me. My friend Bernard took Dylan to a Celtic v. Kilmarnock game at which a Hoops fan was giving me pelters – all the usual stuff about drink and drugs. Bernard sent Dylan for a pie and then had a quiet word in the guy's ear. He told him that he was out of order and that Dylan was my son. The guy never opened his mouth again. Bernard handled that situation well, but it has not always been as straightforward as that. Claire stopped going to games during my days with Kilmarnock because of the constant abuse I was suffering. My mum has refused to watch me again, and that hurts. My brothers have also stopped watching me. They both came within seconds of rolling about the aisles with the idiots giving me pelters, and we decided that it was best they watch another team. It's not fair on them.

On the park, things were going great in my early days with Kilmarnock. I won the SPL Bank of Scotland Player of the Month for August after my blistering start. The cynic in me thought it was just a sympathy vote from the panel, but, looking back, I suppose I did deserve it. Considering the talent in the SPL at that time, guys such as Henrik Larsson, Chris Sutton and Russell Latapy, I was very proud to pick up that award. Didier Agathe also had a great month. He was on a three-month deal at Hibs at that time, after Alex McLeish had taken him from Raith Rovers. O'Neill ended up signing Agathe for Celtic for around £35,000, and it may well have been down to a choice between the two of us. I'd have loved the chance to have played for Celtic.

Martin O'Neill: I was aware of Andy's talent before that game at Parkhead, and he had impressed me. To come to Celtic Park and have the ability and confidence to score a goal like that meant you had the quality to play at a high level. It was a terrific strike and a moment that must have made him very proud, especially after coming through his ordeal earlier that same year. He was a worthy recipient of the accolades he received during that period.

Celtic's interest went no further. In a way, that was probably a good thing, because I felt loyalty towards Bobby, and I signed a three-year contract with Kilmarnock shortly after. The deal was brilliant, and I was on around £2,000 a week. I could have earned more elsewhere, but I was happy where I was and felt good times were ahead at Rugby Park.

Bobby Williamson: Andy was in tremendous form. He scored against Rangers and was looking the part. His goal at Parkhead was a beauty – a rocket into the top corner. Naturally, I was delighted for us to have taken the lead, but then I started to think of the consequences, and thought we'd lose him to another club, because he was attracting lots of attention. We sat him down and gave it our best shot, and he accepted a longer-term contract. It gave the whole club a boost to see him remain at Rugby Park.

Andy had so much natural talent, and he excited the Kilmarnock supporters. He brought fans through the turnstiles in that first season, and he made a valuable contribution. The fact that we didn't pay a penny for him and that we beat a few other SPL teams to get him made it all the sweeter, I suppose. And to be fair to Andy, he made the most of the chance we gave him. Still, if we'd paid a six-figure fee to sign him, we would have had no complaints, as he would have been more than worth it.

Gus MacPherson: When I heard that we had signed Andy, I wondered if we were going to get the Andy who wanted to make a real go of it after all his problems or the Andy who was unable to get rid of his excess baggage. The stories about him when he was on the drink are legendary, and most people in Scottish football were aware of them. I analysed him in his first few days, and, well, it didn't take me long to realise it was the former. When he arrived, he was so eager to impress. He had that initial three-month contract, and it became clear after a week or so that he was going to be handed a lengthy extension. His energy levels were incredible, and he scored a few extraordinary goals – goals only players with above average ability are capable of. Yet he was only four months off the booze when he arrived at our place. Credit to Bobby Williamson for believing Andy had enough drive and determination to resurrect his career.

Andy played a number of games for us on the right wing, and I played behind him at right-back. He had a great level of fitness and always wanted to drop back and help me out. I had to keep telling him to push higher up the park and put the opposing defender under pressure. He was terrific for Kilmarnock and turned out to be an outstanding signing.

Now that I was earning and not pissing it up against a wall, I had the chance to enjoy my money and give my family a better quality of life. We started to go out together for family meals, choosing nice restaurants. It also relieved a few worries I had, as it allowed me to pay off some of the debts that I had accrued during my dark days. I'd taken out one loan after another to pay creditors but had ended up using the money to feed my passion for drink and drugs. I owed a tidy five-figure sum, but I was able to structure my debt in a way that suited the bank and also allowed me to get back on my feet.

The downside of being clean and earning money was that I was always going to be in danger of turning to something else to feed my addictive personality. The danger signs were there, and it was around that time I got back into gambling. I soon became aware that I was spending far too much time at the bookies. I remember one day I put £400 on a horse to win at odds of 5–1. It romped in. I was delighted, although I'd genuinely been shitting myself at putting on such a large amount on one bet. But, like most gamblers, I had more bad days than good ones.

Football dressing-rooms are full of boys who've received tips on this 'certainty' and that 'certainty', and it's easy to get sucked in. I often took the bait when I was at United, but I was drunk and didn't really appreciate what I was doing. Most tips are hopeless and rarely win. I started to lose quite a few quid and needed to take steps to arrest my problem. I never felt as threatened by the gambling as I did with the drink and drugs, but I knew my personality and that I could easily let things get out of control. I had to face up to my growing problem and nip it in the bud. I'd wasted money in the past, and there was no way I was going to put my family through more turmoil. I had no chances left and was enjoying life with them too much to throw it all away.

I'm in control of it now, and it's not like I can't go into a bookies in the way I can't touch a drop of alcohol. I occasionally attended Gamblers Anonymous, mainly to accompany friends of mine who were nervous about going along. Because I'd had experience of AA, they asked me to accompany them, and it was a good way for me to be reminded of the dangers.

I've now restricted myself to the odd bet here and there on the horses and a £20 treble on the football at the weekend. Thankfully, I've deliberately kept myself away from online poker games and the 24-hour access to gambling that's out there these days. It's a dangerous business to get involved in, and I've witnessed at first hand what it can do to people and their lives. Gambling is a completely different beast to drink and drugs, but the consequences can be just as damaging. Drugs and alcohol have a debilitating effect on health, but the psychological effects of gambling are equally devastating.

My form dipped halfway through the season. I suppose that was to be expected. Any winger will tell you that it's hard to play consistently well for more than 40 games and there comes a time when your performance level will shade during a season. It happens to all players. But I was more experienced and tried to do what Jim McLean had told me during my early days at Tannadice. He'd said that there would be days when I wouldn't be playing well, but I still had to make sure the opposition full-back didn't contribute. I might not have been flying past my marker and whipping in cross after cross, but I had to stop the guy I was up against from having a decent game. I felt I was able to do that at Kilmarnock. I had taken on board how to stay involved in a match and contribute to the team even when I wasn't playing well.

Part of the explanation for my slump was that I was doing too much off the park. I agreed to do interview after interview – all about the same thing – and it eventually wore me out. I was doing photo shoots and speaking to magazines, and it was just too much. I should have been resting in the afternoon, but I just couldn't say no to people. When I signed for Kilmarnock, Bobby told me that if I ever needed a few days off, he'd allow it. Apart from one day off to go to an AA meeting, I never took him up on his offer. That was a mistake. I just didn't want to be seen to be receiving any preferential treatment.

Sometime around March, Bobby pulled me into his office after I'd had a couple of bad games on the bounce and told me there was a story doing the rounds that I was back on the booze. I was really upset and told him that it was garbage. He said that he never doubted me. He just wanted to let me know what was being said behind my back by people from outside the club.

Bobby Williamson: Whispering campaigns go on all the time in football. There was one brought to my attention about Andy that he had fallen back into bad habits. I wanted to speak with him about it face to face. I didn't doubt him for a minute, but as a manager you want to allow your player to speak up for himself.

Andy never gave me a moment of bother. To be honest, I never expected him to. He came in, got on with his training and went home. He'd sometimes sit and speak to the younger players, or listen to our more experienced players, and he enjoyed that aspect of our club. We had a happy dressing-room, and that was also part of the reason we achieved a reasonable amount of success that season, finishing fourth and qualifying for the UEFA Cup.

I spoke to Old Chris about the allegations being made about me, and he asked me point blank, 'Have you been drinking?' He knew what the answer was. He then told me that I could not spend the rest of my days worrying about what people might be thinking or saying about me. It was great advice. He was spot on, and his words reminded me of the time I was floored with the flu but still reported for training at Rugby Park. Bobby took one look at me and said, 'What are you doing here looking like this?'

'I'm ill,' I replied. 'I feel terrible. I won't be able to train this morning.'

'I can see that. Get back up the road and get tucked up in bed before you give it to the rest of the boys, you stupid bugger.'

'Sorry, gaffer. I was scared you'd think I'd been drinking at the weekend if I just phoned in without letting you see for yourself. So, you can see this is not drink-related, eh?' It was a learning curve for me.

We reached the CIS League Cup final in my first season at Killie. National boss Craig Brown was supposed to be at the quarter-final with a view to keeping an eye on me for a Scotland call-up. I played well as we defeated Hibs 2–1 on a horrible, wet and windy night. I scored one, set up the other and won the Man of the Match award for my efforts. Normally, the recipient of the award receives a bottle of champagne, but people seem to reckon you're not allowed to give an alcoholic any bevvy. It was funny watching

Killie commercial manager Jim McSherry run about looking for another prize. I won a few Man of the Matches that season and ended up being presented with all sorts, from umbrellas to clocks – anything but champagne! I eventually told Jim that I'd like the bubbly, as I could take it home for Claire to enjoy. Jim was a lovely guy and brilliant at his job. It was typical of him and his staff to be so caring about things like that – they just didn't want to act as if they were cold-hearted.

The CIS Cup semi-final was against St Mirren at Hampden. It was a midweek game, and only about 10,000 spectators turned up. We won 3–0, and I scored with a header at the back post from a Paul Wright cross. Craig Dargo scored a wonder goal when he made a terrific solo run before slotting past Ludovic Roy, and Peter Canero was our other scorer.

Dylan was in the stand that night and sat beside McCoist and Durrant. He had a great time as they wound him up, saying that his dad was a mince footballer. Dylan has great patter of his own, though, and gave as good as he got from the Killie double act. Gus MacPherson came over to me after the game and told me that he was so pleased I'd helped play a part in getting the club to a final. I've never forgotten Gus's kind words that night.

The CIS final wasn't until March, which gave us a few months to prepare ourselves for the game against Celtic. By the time the match arrived, I was off the boil and out of the team. I had an idea I wouldn't be playing but still hoped that Bobby would have faith in me and hand me a starting place. Sadly, my dreams were shattered, and Bobby only gave me a place on the bench. I was gutted.

My head was down before the final, and Bobby came over to assure me that I would get on at some stage. We had a really good squad at the time, and Paul Wright, who had been a brilliant servant to Killie, didn't even make the bench. Martin Baker was also unhappy at not playing, and he threatened to hook Bobby. He was absolutely gutted, and his anger almost boiled over. I don't think he ever got round to it, though!

Celtic were cruising towards the title that season, and the League Cup final was a chance for Martin O'Neill to get his first piece of silverware on board as Parkhead manager. We managed to keep it tight for the first 45 minutes and went in at half-time scoreless, despite the fact that we were dealt a crushing blow when Durranty had to go off injured. Bobby told us to keep it tight for the first ten minutes after the break and then we could open up and go for the win. But Celtic blitzed us in that second 45-minute period, and Henrik Larsson gave a masterclass in striking. They won 3–0, despite Chris Sutton getting a red card, and Larsson scored a hat-trick. It should have been renamed the Larsson final, and it was typical of that season that he won the game for them. He was the difference. I came on in the second half, but there was little we could do to stem the tide.

We managed to keep soldiering on in the SPL and held off Hearts to finish fourth and secure a place in the UEFA Cup. It was a satisfactory end to what had been a good year for me and the club.

I thoroughly enjoyed my first season at Kilmarnock. I scored memorable goals against Celtic, Dundee United, St Johnstone and Rangers. Even if I say so myself, I had been in really good shape up until Christmas and was pleased with my performances.

The hard part was trying to follow that up in my second season. I went away for a great holiday to Florida with Claire and the boys, and I was confident I would be back at Rugby Park a fitter and better player. It didn't work out that way. I felt lethargic and tired most of the time and just couldn't deliver the level of performance I wanted to. I tried to make a contribution in other ways and took it upon myself to speak to the younger players about the dangers of drink and drugs.

In the past, I would have joined the boozers in the dressing-room, but now I avoided the drinkers and the maniacs. I found out what the young boys were like and deliberately befriended the good pros. But, to be fair, there were no bad 'uns in the Killie dressing-room.

Most young players these days are good athletes and have good habits. Sure, they enjoy a night out and a booze, but if they don't strike a balance between work and socialising, they won't last at a good level, or even get there in the first place.

I enjoyed spending time with Jamie Fowler, Paul di Giacomo and Kris Boyd. All three were interested in why I had gone off the rails and took on board my advice about the pitfalls of being a young professional. I could tell Boydy was as daft as me in terms of wanting a carry-on and a good time, but he knew when to screw the nut. I'm happy he got his move to Rangers and has won caps for Scotland.

Bobby left to join Hibs towards the end of my second season. Hibs had lost Alex McLeish to Rangers and replaced him with Franck Sauzée. Things didn't work out for Sauzée, and Hibs were flirting with relegation. The Easter Road board opted for Bobby to come in, and it made sense. He had an excellent record at Kilmarnock and knew exactly what was required to stabilise an SPL club and then kick on from there.

I was sad to see Bobby go. He saved my career, more or less. But I wasn't in the Killie team at the time and part of me believed a new manager would mean a fresh start for me and a chance to get back in the first team. To be honest, Bobby had been right not to play me, as I didn't deserve to be in the team. But being a typical footballer, I got it into my head that it was the manager's fault and little to do with me.

Jim Jefferies was appointed as Bobby's successor. Jim had a fantastic record at Falkirk and Hearts, and had taken the Jambos to a Scottish Cup victory in 1998 after defeating Rangers in the final. He had a short spell at Bradford that didn't quite work out for him, but I'm sure that had more to do with financial issues than his abilities as a manager.

We hosted Dundee in Jim's first game in charge. It was bedlam before the game, as there had been a car crash on the A77 in which someone had been killed. The road was closed off by police, which meant a huge detour for me to make it to Kilmarnock. What was normally no more than a thirty-five-minute journey from home to the stadium took two hours. Jim was constantly phoning me to ask where I was and if I'd be on time to play. The kick-off was delayed by about 20 minutes. I didn't arrive until 2.45 p.m., and Jim named me as a sub.

We were losing 2–1 when the new boss told me to get ready. I went on and scored two to help us win 3–2. One of my goals was a left-foot volley, and the other was a header in the last minute. I wound up the boys in the dressing-room afterwards and told them that I'd just start turning up every week at a quarter to three!

Billy Brown was Jim's assistant, and he had a good chat with me after the game. He wanted to know why I hadn't been starting every week. I was honest and told him that it was all down to me. I simply wasn't playing well enough when I was given a chance on a match day or doing the business in training to merit a start.

Like Bobby, Clarky and Cabey before them, I took to Jim and Billy. Sure, they could growl and shout from the touchline, but they just wanted to see us win every game.

The 2002–03 season was the final year of my contract, and I was desperate to do well so that I could either earn a new deal at Killie or at least put myself in the shop window and attract interest from elsewhere. Things were going fine until I injured my shoulder in a league game against Partick Thistle at Rugby Park. I got into a tangle with wee Alex Burns and landed awkwardly. I felt my right shoulder pop out and then pop back in again as I rolled over. It was agony.

The problem with being injured was that Jim would always start ranting about players in the modern era who fall down too easily, saying that we were all a bunch of poofs. Jim was from the old school and reckoned the present crop of players wouldn't have lasted five minutes in his era. He loved telling us the story of how he'd played on in a game for Hearts when one of his toes was virtually hanging off. It had been bandaged up, and he had carried on when he should have been in hospital getting it sorted.

However, my shoulder gave me serious problems, and I was booked into Crosshouse Hospital in Kilmarnock for an MRI scan. I hated it – it felt like I was lying in a coffin. I entered head first, and my legs dangled out the end. I suffer from claustrophobia, so 50 minutes in there felt like an eternity. I had a panic button, and I was close to pressing it a couple of times. Patients were allowed to take in their own CD for comfort, but it didn't help my anxiety.

Eventually, the results came back, and the docs told me that I had to have an operation. If I'd avoided surgery, my shoulder might have popped in and out on a regular basis. I was told it could take up to one year after the operation before I'd be fit enough to play football again. With my contract up at the end of the season, that was the worst possible news.

I had to wear a cast across my shoulder, which made life awkward. I couldn't even wash myself properly in that area, and I remember the smell wasn't too pleasant around my armpit! I hated being injured and sitting about doing absolutely nothing, so I was determined to prove the doc's diagnosis wrong. Don't ask me how I did it, but I was back playing ten or eleven weeks after the scan. I trained again for the first time on a Thursday, and Billy asked me if I could play on the Saturday against Partick Thistle. I thought he was kidding. He wasn't. I played at Firhill, but we lost 3–0. Jim was raging and called us in for training on the Sunday morning as a punishment.

The hard-line strategy must have worked, as we went on an unbeaten run after that. In my usual fashion, I told the boys that it was all down to my return – Andy McLaren had managed to dig them out of a hole once again!

My contract was nearly up, and there was interest from a few clubs. Bobby got in touch to ask if I'd be interested in moving to

Hibs. Working with Bobby again appealed to me, as did playing for Hibs, a club I regarded as being one of the best in Scottish football and bigger than Kilmarnock. But Jim and Billy were keen for me to stay and said they'd urge the board to give me the best possible offer. It seemed I was in a great position, and I thought I couldn't lose.

Killie made me an offer, which was, from memory, around about 20 per cent less than what I was on. The ball had more or less burst in Scottish football by that point, and a lot of players had to take wage cuts. Looking back, I should have stayed at Kilmarnock and put pen to paper on the two-year deal that was on offer. But I chased the money.

I don't have a problem admitting that at that stage of my career money was my motivation, and I believed I was good enough to earn more than what was on offer from my current employer. I knew that I had no more than five years left at a high level and wanted to maximise my earning potential. I had a mortgage to pay and mouths to feed. I wanted to put as much away as I could to make life as comfortable as possible when I retired from full-time football.

Jim Jefferies: When I took over at Kilmarnock, I had a good look at the squad I inherited, and I was pleased to be given the chance to work with Andy. He was a player who interested me when I was managing at other clubs, and I'd thought about signing him. For one reason or another, it never happened. He scored two goals to help me win my first game in charge, and I knew he'd do for me. It was just unfortunate I didn't get the chance to work with him longer.

I rated Andy as a player. He was an out-and-out winner, although he could take things a little too far on the pitch, and we had to take him off a few times before he got himself sent off. He was also a good lad to have in the dressing-room. In fact, one of our younger laddies at the club was having some problems in his private life, and Andy volunteered to take him aside and have a wee chat with him. It worked a treat, as the boy gradually started to straighten himself out.

The contract we offered Andy was on reduced terms. It was the start of a new business plan at the club, and there was little room for negotiation. He decided to reject our offer and move elsewhere. I wanted him to stay, as I knew he'd be good for two more years. We had to look for another player, and it wasn't as if we had more money than we had offered to Andy. If anything, we probably had less money to work with.

I said to Billy that we'd miss Andy. And we did. We missed his work rate and ability, and also missed the fact he had no fear when he was out on the pitch. He loved to take men on and whip the ball into the box. We're still in touch, and I hope he looks back on his time with Billy and me fondly.

Ian Durrant: It was a crying shame when Andy left Kilmarnock – a real sad day. I realise he had to look for the best deal possible for him and his family, but he was a loss to the dressing-room and to the team.

He had a great three years at the club, yet it had been a gamble for Bobby to sign him. Andy had been in the very early stages of battling against many, many demons, and nobody knew for sure if he'd come through it all unscathed. After a few training sessions, I could see that he was a really talented player. I enjoyed having Andy as a teammate, as I knew that when I got the ball he would always be available. He never hid and always demanded the ball, which was a dream for a player like me.

In the dressing-room, he was completely infectious. He could also be a pain in the arse, but a funny pain in the arse. Wee Craig Dargo used to be on the receiving end of Andy's one-liners. Ally 'Wee Bully' Mitchell would often pick up Andy to take him to training, and Dargo would already be in the car, sitting in the front seat. Andy would slaughter Dargo the whole journey, and it used to leave Wee Bully stressed. The journey was like the Cannonball Run. *It was priceless. When they all arrived at 9.45 a.m., Dargo was ready to fight Andy. They'd get into the dressing-room, and I'd be ready to pick up the baton from Andy. It would be my turn to give Dargo some verbal pelters.*

It was all good-natured stuff. The Kilmarnock dressing-room at that time was different class. Myself and Coisty were in it, but we were coming to the end of our careers. Bobby recognised that the dressing-room was going to need one or two characters to take over, and Andy fitted the jigsaw perfectly.

I kept a wee eye on him when he first arrived, because I can relate to boys from Glasgow and want to see them make the best of their lives. We found ourselves in each other's company more and more. We had great fun together, and we just pick up from where we left off if we ever meet. Andy is a gem of a guy. Yes, he's made mistakes, but we all have. That shouldn't detract from all the positives he brings.

I miss that Kilmarnock dressing-room. Being a coach is great fun, and it has many good points, but you can't beat being in a dressing-room. It's like your own wee empire, and Andy was a major part of that.

There was no fall out with Killie, but I took Bobby up on his offer and headed to Easter Road. What a complete and utter waste of time that was. I was treated appallingly. I trained with Hibs for the best part of six weeks and played in pre-season games, including high-profile ones such as the Festival Cup against Hearts and a match away at Preston. I was playing well, and my fitness was at a decent level. Bobby was really pleased with me. So where was my contract offer? I waited and waited but nothing happened. I travelled through to Edinburgh every day during pre-season but didn't receive a penny. And as I made my way along the M8 each day, I got angrier and angrier. I didn't want to rock the boat in case it jeopardised any contract negotiations, but I was really pissed off with Hibs' attitude towards me. 'Just keep quiet,' I'd say to myself. 'It'll work out in the end.'

The closest I got to a deal was when Bobby pulled me aside

two days before Hibs' opening league game of the season against Dundee United and told me he wanted me to play. But there was no contract to go with his request. All that was on offer was travelling expenses and the win bonus if we took the three points. I felt sick to my stomach. It was as though I'd had the piss taken out of me and had been used. Bobby obviously knew I was good enough to get a game, but the club didn't think I deserved a contract. I knew Bobby's hands were tied, and, to be frank, I believe he was embarrassed about the way I was treated.

I told Bobby that there was no way I was accepting his offer to play against Dundee United and that I had no option but to look for another club. I'd been clean for more than three years by that stage. I'd successfully managed to fight my daily battle against alcohol, but the whole episode with Hibs really messed me up. It messed me up so much that it almost drove me back on the bevvy. That Thursday night, I thought about going into an off-licence and buying a few beers. At that time, it seemed the best way to escape from the way I'd been treated by Hibs. I felt I had no energy to battle on.

I didn't sleep that night, and Claire was concerned about my state of mind. I spoke to her and a couple of the lads in AA to calm me down, and they tried to make me see sense.

Friday was another day, and I felt in decent shape. I was going to phone every manager I could get a number for and ask them for a game the next day. I was going to show Hibs that they'd made a huge mistake by not offering me a deal.

Bobby Williamson: I wanted to sign Andy. We needed proven SPL players, and I knew he would do well for us. However, Hibs wouldn't back me on it. They said it was down to cash, but I knew Andy wouldn't have been too difficult to deal with. I knew he wanted to play for Hibs, but we didn't even put an offer on the table for him to consider. I was disappointed for him. He looked good in pre-season and worked really hard to show he'd be an asset to us. It was a blow to lose him.

I spoke to John Hughes at Falkirk in the afternoon, and he offered me a place on the bench, as he had already named his starting line-up. Falkirk played their games at Stenhousemuir's Ochilview Stadium that season, and I was a sub for the game against Inverness Caledonian Thistle.

Scott McKenzie picked up an injury early in the game and was taken off. I slotted into his position in the centre of midfield alongside Russell Latapy. Russell and I both like to get on the ball, but we're not really renowned for tracking back. I don't think that either of us made a tackle all day, but somehow we emerged 2–1 winners.

By that point, word was out that I was looking for a club, and I received good press for my performance against Inverness. I always think it's easier to get a move in the summer than it is in the January transfer window. The sun is shining, every player has a wee bit of colour about them and the pitches are in great condition to play football on.

Several clubs made contact with my agent, and the ones that made me sit up and take notice were Aberdeen, Motherwell, Dundee United and Carlisle, who had been taken over by an Irish consortium and were spending decent money to get the club out of the English Third Division. Kilmarnock also got back in touch to say they'd still take me back. The four SPL clubs had all got off to a stuttering start on the first day of the season and perhaps early panic and fear of relegation set in.

Dougie Vipond came to my house that week to interview me for *Sportscene*. It was a lovely day, and the cameraman set up in our back garden. Tyler was running about daft, playing football in the background, trying to sneak himself onto telly. During the interview, I received phone calls from Aberdeen and Dundee United.

Steve Paterson was in charge of the Dons at the time, and I'd spoken to him a few times in the past. He'd had his problems with alcohol, and when it had become public knowledge, I'd phoned him to say that if he needed any advice or just a different voice to listen to, I'd always, at the very least, be on the end of the phone for him. I didn't contact him to be nosey, I was just showing some concern, as I knew what a tough time he'd be having.

Steve wanted a right winger and asked if I'd be interested in moving north. Money was tight at Pittodrie, but he told me he was trying to squeeze some cash out of his board to make me as attractive an offer as possible. But I spoke to Claire about the prospect of moving up there, and we had reservations about it.

Maurice Malpas was assistant manager at Motherwell and a former teammate at Dundee United. He phoned my agent to say that he was keen to take me to Fir Park, and his interest put me on a high. When we played together, Maurice was a moany bastard, but, to be fair to him, he only had words with you for the right reasons. His criticisms were always constructive. I was just too young and naive at that time to appreciate what he was trying to do for me. He was a senior professional at United when I was there and had the best interests of the young players at heart. He was a top player and hardly any winger got the better of him. We were never friendly – never connected on a sense-of-humour level. I know my attitude had him shaking his head in disbelief more often than not, and I'm probably the main reason he's bald!

I was flattered that a number of prominent SPL clubs still reckoned I could do a job for them. In the end, though, I chose to go back to Tannadice. Ian McCall wanted me, and I received a very good offer from him. Like I said, I chased the money.

They say that you should never go back, and in hindsight I realise that I should not have returned to United. I had knocked Paul Sturrock back three years earlier because of my memories of when I'd hit the road to self-destruction in Dundee, and the correct decision this time round would have been to stay with Kilmarnock. Even after I left to go to Hibs for that ill-fated pre-season spell, Killie still kept in touch. Billy Brown was on the phone on a regular basis to be kept up to date. At the end of each conversation, he used to say, 'Don't forget, Andy, you can still come back here.'

There's no doubt that I was tempted, but how could I return to a dressing-room three months after walking out? What would the fans have said? Perhaps I was frightened of losing face after having knocked them back. I also had great memories of playing there – without doubt, the happiest times of my career as a footballer. I had the pleasure of meeting some fabulous people and playing with such guys as McCoist and Durrant.

McCoist was approaching the end of his career, but he was still a top-drawer goalscorer. Once a genius, always a genius – at least, that's what he used to tell us! To be honest, after his illustrious career at Rangers, I thought he was probably at Rugby Park for a bit of a jolly – a top-up for his pension. I couldn't have been more wrong.

A game against Dunfermline in which we were trailing at half-time after turning in a woeful first-half performance gives an insight into his professionalism and dedication. Coisty came in and absolutely ripped into us all. He told us that we were a disgrace and had to up it a level. He'd obviously played in more important games than that one, but that wasn't the point as far as he was concerned. The bottom line was that he was a winner and wouldn't tolerate anything less than 100 per cent from his teammates. I was impressed with his hunger and desire. We went on to win the game in the second half.

He didn't train with us too often, but when he was there he was totally professional and an inspiration to us all. He was a great finisher, and his movement was so clever. He didn't waste energy – he only moved when it was worthwhile. He's a lovely person – a really infectious guy with an incredible knack of making time for everybody and squeezing so much into his packed diary.

I enjoyed my time at Kilmarnock – it was the best and happiest period of my career – but I left the club, and that was a mistake. I should have stayed, but hindsight is a wonderful thing, and I can't change what happened now.

12

CAPPING OFF MY REHABILITATION

I WAS in the house when the phone rang. 'Hello, is that Andy?'

'Aye. Who's this?'

'It's Craig Brown here. Just to let you know, I've called you up for the forthcoming Scotland friendly in Poland.'

'Pardon?'

'It's Craig Br . . .'

'Right. I'm not falling for that old one. Who is this?'

It was Craig Brown, and he was phoning to let me know that I had been included in the senior Scotland squad. I couldn't believe it. I was lost for words.

The reason I was sceptical when Craig phoned was that I'd been caught out by that kind of thing before. When I was at United, I got a phone call from one of the youth-team players pretending to be an SFA official. He said that I'd been called up for the Scotland Under-21 squad, and I fell for it. Totally. It was only when the guy couldn't control himself any longer and started to laugh that he gave the game away.

This time, however, it was for real, and I was so proud. It was also great that Claire and the boys were home to share the good news with me. Old Jimmy from AA had also popped in just before Craig phoned, which was appropriate, because Jimmy told me just after I joined AA that I would be back in full-time football within a few months and playing for Scotland within a year. Naturally, I thought

159

he was potty, but he was absolutely right. He had more faith in me than I had in myself.

I wasn't selected in Brown's original squad for the Poland game, but that didn't matter to me. I couldn't care less how I made it. The squad had several call-offs, and Brown was forced to bring in replacements. As a result, Barry Nicholson, Stevie Crawford, John O'Neil and Charlie Miller were also drafted in for the journey to Bydgoszcz.

Craig Brown: Andy didn't believe me when I called him, and I was happy about that. It meant his feet were on the ground and he'd be ready to take the game seriously and put in a shift when required.

I was given less than 24 hours' notice to meet up with the squad, and the schedule was so tight that I ended getting changed into my official blazer and trousers on the team bus on the way to the airport. When we arrived, I roomed with Stevie Caldwell, who was quite a quiet lad. I was more interested in playing cards in wee Charlie's room. We were in and out of Poland in one night, but that was still long enough to win a few bob from a couple of the lads at three-card brag.

Initially, Craig Brown and the SFA received some stick for taking the game on. Of course, when some of the established players pulled out of the squad on the eve of the journey abroad, there was even more criticism. In fact, Roger Mitchell, the SPL chief executive at that time, described it as a 'diddy international'. I couldn't have cared less if the game was in the back of beyond against a team of pen-pushers or waiters. When I was in the changing-room putting on my Scotland jersey, I felt so proud.

I was disappointed not to start, but I respected and understood Brown's team selection. I came on at half-time for Colin Cameron with the score at 0–0. We went a goal down when Radoslaw Kaluzny scored with a close-range header in the 49th minute. I almost equalised, but one of the Polish players cleared my shot off the line. We were then awarded a penalty in the 69th minute when Scott Booth was fouled inside the box by Kaluzny. I immediately had the ball in my hands and was desperate to take the spot-kick.

Booth came running over and told me that Craig had said he was to take it. It wasn't for me to disobey orders when playing for my country, especially on my debut. I must have been feeling shy that night! Although Scott still had to give the ball a bit of a tug to wrestle it from me. Thankfully, he didn't let us down, and we came away from Poland with a creditable 1–1 draw. To achieve a draw away from home was satisfactory. We actually played quite well and received favourable reports from the Scottish papers the next day.

On the flight home, I sat alone and was actually quite glad of the solitude. It gave me a chance to reflect on an incredible 12-month spell. To go from where I had been a year earlier to playing for Scotland was incredible. Some people suggest that Craig only gave me a game as a bit of a sympathy vote. However, I don't believe he did. I had played really well that season and deserved my chance. OK, the squad was decimated with injuries and I wasn't a first pick. But did I care? My solitary cap in Poland meant I'd represented my country at every level in the game, and I'm so proud of that. I will remember 25 April 2001 until the day I die.

Craig Brown: Andy deserved his cap. He was not selected so there would be some sort of romantic story attached to it all. I'd known Andy since he was 15, and I liked him from day one. I was saddened to see his demise in the game when he was drinking far too heavily, but credit to him for owning up to it all and seeking professional help. I can say in my heart of hearts that there was no sentiment involved in his call-up for that game. I have to admit that you feel embarrassed to award an international cap to some players, but that was not the case with Andy.

He had power, strength, a change of pace and good control. He also had an ability to run at defenders and take them on. And for a player who operated in wide areas, he was brave – totally fearless. Defenders hated playing against him, because he was not the type to run and hide after they'd whacked him.

Andy would have won an international cap sooner had he led a different lifestyle off the park, although part of his problem was that he was just too inconsistent. From early in his career, he had a reputation as a player who needed to be 'managed'.

Andy was a bit of a rebel. When Paul Sturrock was in charge of the youth team at Dundee United, he would often phone me up, sounding as though he was at the end of his tether and asking how he could keep control of Andy and big Duncan Ferguson. Paul thought that he'd have to chain them to the main door at Tannadice to have any chance of keeping them under control.

But Andy was always receptive to advice and a good listener. He was like that from when Ross Mathie had him in his Under-16 squad for the 1989 World Cup finals. Ross enjoyed working with Andy.

I suppose I didn't expect to play for Scotland again. I knew I was only a stopgap. Craig was always loyal to the players who had served him well over the years, and I never had a problem with that. However, when Berti Vogts took over from Craig after our failure to qualify for the 2002 World Cup finals in Japan and South Korea, he pretty much ripped the squad apart and brought in dozens of new faces. To be honest, players with nowhere near the ability I possessed were being selected and selected regularly. If I had been a couple of years younger when Vogts took over, or if he had been in charge during my good form at Kilmarnock, I reckon I might well have reached double figures for Scotland. There were guys during that period who we all know were not good enough to wear the dark blue of Scotland.

Vogts had some horrendous results, and the malaise on the park was reflected in the mood of the nation. Scotland takes pride in the game of football, and under Vogts we were turning into a laughing stock. Our results were awful, and I'm sure that if he had been an SPL manager, he would have been sacked long before the SFA decided to take action. His methods and style of management were called into question by fans and pundits up and down the country, and it wasn't just the Tartan Army who were baffled. Players in every professional dressing-room in Scotland wanted to know what the problem was. I remember during that depressing period the subject of Vogts and his tactical failures were constantly talked about between players and their respective coaches at club level.

By that point, however, I'd thankfully managed to live the dream and play for my country. And in the end, I'm happy with my lot. After all I've been through off the park, to have my name in the history books as a Scotland player is something I'll always cherish, and it can never be taken away from me.

13

BACK TAY WHERE IT ALL STARTED

I SIGNED a contract with Dundee United in August 2003. The deal, initially for one month, was verbally agreed in Owen Coyle's house in the south side of Glasgow. Owen was player–coach and outlined the plans United boss Ian McCall had for the club.

I had played with Owen at Tannadice a few years earlier, and he was aware of my reluctance to stay in Dundee and the baggage that I was carrying. He told me that the club was completely different from how it had been back then and that there were new people in the boardroom with new ideas. And I could still stay in Glasgow, as a few lads travelled up to Tannadice every day. McCall also played his part in persuading me to sign during my meeting in Owen's house. The gaffer was in Tayside that day but was in constant contact with Owen, who would pass me the phone on a regular basis.

United had lost every one of their first three league games playing with a 3–5–2 system. Scott Paterson had picked up an injury, and they had no proper cover for him, so they wanted to switch to a 4–4–2 formation. The problem was that United had no one to play wide on the right of midfield. They told me that I was the man to solve the problem.

During the meeting, I received a call on my mobile from Phil McTaggart, a member of John Viola's staff. Phil informed me that the Spanish side Córdoba CF had replied to a fax and videotape of me in action that he'd sent them. I couldn't speak in front of Owen and told Phil I'd phone him back in half an hour. I was excited to find out more about this interest from Spain and, to be honest, couldn't wait to get out of Owen's house. I reckon Owen knew something might be going down, and he was determined to not let me leave without a handshake, at least, on a deal.

Córdoba were in the Spanish Second Division and were on the lookout for a wide right player. They were impressed with my ability, and the discussions had reached the stage of me being verbally offered a one-year contract, worth in the region of £100,000 per year, plus a car and house. I told Phil that I was up for it and to try and advance the deal.

I spoke to Claire, and before we knew it we had the sombreros, the suntan lotion and the Julio Iglesias CD looked out! Córdoba is on the Spanish south coast, and they had real ambitions to win promotion to *La Liga*. I was keen for a deal to be signed and sealed. Claire and the boys would move out with me, and the worst-case scenario was that we'd have had a nine-month holiday in Spain.

The only time there had been a chance for me to play abroad before was when I was told Borussia Dortmund were impressed by my performance for Scotland against Germany in an Under-18 game. Murdo MacLeod was at Dortmund at that time and had made a good impression. The club must have thought that it wasn't a bad idea to consider more Scots. One of the Borussia coaching staff was in charge of that German national youth side, and he was hugely impressed with me. I was unaware of it, but Craig Brown told me about a year later that Murdo had informed him that Dortmund had raved about me and I had been under consideration.

Nothing came of it, unfortunately, and my proposed move to Córdoba also fell through. They decided to pursue other options. So, instead of being by the water in Marbella, I ended up by the sea in Broughty Ferry.

There was a lack of confidence at United when I joined. The team had lost the first few games of the season, so I walked into the dressing-room on my first day and boldly declared, 'Right, lads. Panic over!' I've never been shy, and that was my idea of breaking the ice. Derek McInnes was the captain, and we didn't really know each other. He later told me that it was the best opening line he'd ever heard from a player.

Derek McInnes: Andy walked in and, as bold as you like, announced he'd have us in the top six by Christmas. I'd never played with him, but after a couple of training sessions I could see he'd been coached well and had natural ability. He was a great signing for United. To get an established striker in for no transfer fee was tremendous business. He was always a goal threat and just loved getting the ball and running at defenders.

He'd have his daft head on quite a lot, but Andy knew when to be serious, and he gave his all in training and in games. He played a huge part for us that season with his goals and also helped the younger players settle in. He took an interest in the players just starting out in the professional game, and they responded positively to him. He was a good person to have around the dressing-room and a great player to have on the pitch.

The Andy McLaren that returned to play for Dundee United was a totally different person to the one that had left four years earlier. I was in good shape, and I was enjoying my profession again.

My debut was against Livingston, and we drew 0–0. It was our first point of the season. We then had a midweek CIS Cup game at home to Morton, and we won 3–1. I scored one and set one up. It was then that I agreed a three-year contract with United. McCall was desperate for me to sign, as he knew other clubs were sniffing about.

The main reason I joined United was for the money – I won't try to bullshit and say that it was for any other reason. They offered me a three-year deal worth £1,700 per week, plus £400 appearance money and a £5,000 signing on fee. I was 29 at that time and thought that it could well be my last major deal in the game. I'd never made the £10,000 a week that people automatically think most footballers earn, and I had wasted most of the money that I had made. This was my chance to earn some decent cash for a few years and to continue to play football at a good level.

I also thought I was worth that kind of money and wasn't being greedy. Perhaps I got a wee bit above myself, but I knew what some players in the SPL were earning – outwith the Old Firm – and I felt that I was entitled to a piece of the action after the way I had performed for Killie for two out of the three seasons I'd been there. So I followed the pound signs. I was happy.

Owen Coyle: Andy had baggage, but I'm a believer that people deserve a second chance. After admitting to his problems and having such a good spell at Kilmarnock, it was clear that Andy was serious about helping himself and tackling his demons. In order for him to continue leading a good life, he needed help from other people. He felt let down a little bit that summer, after what had happened to him elsewhere, and that worked in our favour.

He was a breath of fresh air at United, as I knew he would be. Other clubs must have been disappointed that they didn't go that extra wee bit to get him when he was doing so well for us.

I knew that travelling up and down every day to Dundee from Glasgow might get to me, but I thought the money would ease any discomfort from the daily 170-mile round trip. And we went on to have a terrific season, finishing fifth in the SPL. We improved as a team, and I was really pleased with my contribution. I played up front alongside Jim McIntyre, and we just hit it off. We used to cause defenders all sorts of problems, and the team became a real force at home. Tannadice became a bit of a fortress again, and we went on an unbeaten run that lasted at least six months. I think only Celtic and Rangers won more points in that period than we did.

We also defeated Rangers 2–0 at Tannadice, and I scored with a header. It was a terrific result. People can say what they like about Rangers at that time – yes, Celtic won the league comfortably – but Alex McLeish still had a good side. Frank de Boer played for them, and he was an outstanding footballer – one of the best defenders I ever faced.

During my career, I enjoyed some good moments against Rangers. People said that was because I'm a Celtic fan and I tried harder against the men from Ibrox. Utter garbage. I tried my best against both sides, as I loved the buzz of playing against the Old Firm. I'm a professional footballer, and playing in front of at least 50,000 people in their backyard is what it's all about. I used to sit in the dressing-room ready to play against the Old Firm and could see the fear in the eyes of some of my teammates. I knew that they didn't have the mental strength to cope with the big occasion. They were beaten before a ball was kicked. I just didn't get that. I wanted to play in front of huge crowds in packed grounds every week. But sometimes I took my enthusiasm too far and ended up done in before I'd even left the dressing-room. I was so hyper and wound up, I was pretty much knackered by the time I got out onto the pitch.

It happened to me during my final season at Kilmarnock in 2003 when the title race between Rangers and Celtic went down to the wire. We played Rangers at Ibrox, and they needed to win to stay ahead of Celtic. I had it all planned in my head: I was going to ruin their day. I was going to silence 50,000 pumped-up Rangers fans and hog the back-page headlines the next morning. I ran out onto the pitch, and Ibrox was the noisiest I'd ever heard it. It was unbelievable. I wondered how Rangers could fail with such incredible backing from the stands, and I blew it. I took my mental preparation too far and couldn't get going. I also had a run-in with Fernando Ricksen, and I was basically no good to Kilmarnock that day. Jim Jefferies gave me the hook at half-time, and he was right to do so. I hated the feeling that I'd let myself and my club down on the big stage. There's nothing worse than being at Ibrox or Parkhead and looking up at the scoreboard to see that you're two goals down after twenty minutes. You think, 'Oh, fuck. It's going to be a long day!'

We lost 5–0 to Rangers that day, and they went on to win the title on goal difference on the last day of the season. But on that occasion, and every other time I played against either of the Old Firm sides, I was never once in a dressing-room when the manager asked us to play for a 0–0 draw. It was suicide to go down that road. I've even gone to Parkhead and Ibrox and played in a team with three up front.

But we hardly got into the opposition box that afternoon, because we just couldn't get the ball. And when we did, we struggled to string three passes together. Some managers would tell you to keep it tight and not do anything silly for the first ten minutes. You could then try to take it on from there. But I always believed that any side I was playing in could win every game. My mates would phone me before we played against Celtic or Rangers and ask how many we were going to lose by. I never entertained them and said I fancied us to win. We rarely did, but some of them made a tidy sum from the bookies on the odd occasion when we made a mockery of the odds.

Credit should go to Ian McCall and his coaching staff for the team playing so well that year. Our success was all the more remarkable because the club had financial problems at that time, and the players were asked to defer all bonus and appearance money for about two thirds of the season. We could have fought the club and not given 100 per cent, but we decided to go with it and all do our bit to help United through their mini-crisis. We weren't totally convinced that we'd be squared up at the end of the season, but fair play to owner Eddie Thompson. He sorted the boys out with what they were due, and I picked up a nice cheque in the region of £15,000 that summer from the deferred payments.

I came back for pre-season feeling good and desperate to take off from the previous campaign. I had a good four or five weeks' preparation for the first SPL game of the season, away to Dunfermline. However, McCall snubbed me for that game. I wasn't even named as a sub. It came out of the blue. He gave me no indication that it was on his mind to leave me in the stand. He'd signed James Grady in the summer, and I realised that the new boy would be favourite to start. But to be bombed completely was a real kicking. McCall named his side just over an hour before kick-off, and I walked out of the dressing-room at East End Park absolutely distraught. To train all week and then have nothing to show for it come the weekend was too much for me to take.

The weeks passed, and there was no sign of any light at the end of the tunnel. Tannadice became a dark place, and I started to slip into a state of depression. The travelling became a chore, and I stopped going to AA meetings. I wasn't taking care of my mind. There's an old saying in AA that we 'get our medicine through our ears', and I'd stopped getting my fix. My head wasn't right. I felt fucked. Being left out of the team triggered it all off. I've no doubt about that.

I also became terrible to live with again. Claire always said I was a pain in the backside with a drink down me. Sober or not, she didn't like this Andy, either – the one who shouted at our sons for next to no reason and picked arguments with her when she was guilty of nothing.

Thinking there was no chance of McCall selecting me, my head really went down after a few weeks of that season. If I had been attending my meetings, it would have helped me to knuckle down in training, but not even that avenue was open to me. All the shite that happened in my childhood started to eat away inside my head again. I had no escape from my mental torture. Not being able to play was having a huge and devastating psychological effect on me. It came to a head one day in training when I had a panic attack. We were playing a bounce game when all of a sudden

I found it difficult to breathe. I felt like I was suffocating, and I thought I was going to collapse. It was, I suppose, a culmination of a number of things: the depression of not playing and also the fact that I wasn't sleeping well. I was tossing and turning at four in the morning. I'd then drive up to Dundee for a day's work on the back of about two hours' sleep.

I went to my local GP in Glasgow and told him what had been going on. He prescribed a course of Valium. I told McCall and the United medical staff, and they were fine about it. I wasn't too sure about taking the medication, but I wasn't going to argue with the doc's prescription. I needed to try something to get my life and career back on track. United wanted to keep the whole thing quiet, and I was happy to agree.

However, what I couldn't hide from was the fact that I needed a change. An offer came in for me to go out on loan and play in the First Division for Partick Thistle, the club having been relegated from the SPL the season before. Gerry Britton and Derek Whyte were in charge at that time. My United career was going down the toilet, and a move to Firhill seemed like the lifeline I needed. But sadly my move to Maryhill was a disaster. Thistle were in freefall, and I hardly played for them. I was there for about 11 games and started only once. Gerry and Derek were dismissed shortly afterwards.

The Jags' 'Messiah', John Lambie, came back to take temporary charge, and he led them to a 2–1 win against Falkirk. It was some result as Falkirk won the league that year. I went back to United and things didn't improve. I was stuck in the reserves, and I was frustrated. I then had an argument with McCall at the end of a reserve game about comments he made in the dressing-room.

Not long after, I was named as a sub for a game against Dundee. We were losing, and as I warmed up behind one of the goals the United fans chanted my name, desperate to see me go on to try to turn the game in our favour. McCall left me on the bench.

Another loan move was just around the corner. Morton came

in for me in the February of that season. I didn't fancy dropping down to the Second Division, but anything had to be better than what I was going through at Tannadice. The positive thing was that the club were going for promotion. They were managed by my former United teammate Jim McInally, and the journey down the M8 to Greenock from Glasgow was no problem.

Derek McInnes: United missed Andy that season, no doubts. Personally, I missed him, and I think the atmosphere in the dressing-room suffered due to his absence. We travelled together to Dundee every day, and he made the journey much more bearable. The car journey up the road could get you down, and there were days you just could not be bothered with the trek to Dundee, but after a few minutes in the car with Andy it didn't seem as bad. The minutes just flew in. His patter was great, and he was fun when he had his daft head on.

The only problem was when we made the journey in Andy's car. Andy liked a cigarette, and some days he would puff quite a few. The smell wasn't the greatest, and we used to joke that it wasn't a sunroof he had in his car, it was a chimney! We had to have the windows down and even the air freshener was trying to escape!

My debut game for Morton was against Stranraer, and I scored two goals. I had another disallowed when the assistant referee flagged for offside. I was never offside. That decision cost me the first hat-trick of my career. But, more importantly, the three points kept us in the hunt for promotion. That win put us eight points behind Stranraer. Brechin ran away with the league that season, but the battle for second spot went down to the wire. We travelled to Stair Park for the second-last game of the season needing a win. We could only manage a 1–1 draw, and that was our chance of automatic promotion gone. Around 3,000 Morton fans travelled to Stranraer for the game, and I was gutted for them that we didn't get the right result. After the match, I took my top off and gave it to a young boy who attended all the games.

The Morton fans wanted me to sign permanently for the club, but at that time I wasn't sure. I suppose I still thought I could do a job for United in the SPL. By that point, McCall had been sacked and his assistant Gordon Chisholm had taken over on a caretaker basis with a view to landing the job permanently.

United had won a place in the Scottish Cup final against Celtic, and I was eligible to play at Hampden. My season with Morton finished three weeks before the cup final, and I should have gone back to United to train in the hope of forcing my way into the manager's plans. But there was no contact from Chisholm or any other member of his staff. I took that to mean that I was surplus to requirements for the rest of the season.

I went along to the team hotel in East Kilbride on the morning of the final at Hampden. I wanted to give my support to the players and the club. However, I felt like a total stranger and was really uncomfortable. I got the impression that a Celtic player would have been made to feel more welcome than I was. I'd been at Dundee United for 11 years but felt as though I'd never stepped foot inside the club. United didn't even have a ticket for me, and I was ready to walk away and see if one of my mates had a spare one for the Celtic end, but one of the United medical staff gave me one of his briefs.

Celtic won the final 1–0. It was a scrappy game – not a memorable cup final by any stretch of the imagination. As Celtic started to parade the cup on the lap of honour, I disappeared out of Hampden and headed home. I knew at that moment I'd never play for United again.

I returned to the club for pre-season training after Chisholm sent me a letter asking me to report early. I thought he was going to try and fuck me about by getting me to train twice a day – with the first session in the morning and the last session at night – but it was just to sort out a pay-off. Chisholm wanted me to take a settlement for the remaining year of my contract. It took a couple of weeks to sort out, but we got there eventually. Meanwhile, McInally had kept on at me to go back to Morton, and I signed a two-year contract with the club.

I was hurt at the way it had ended at United. I'd given them eleven years during my two spells and was due a testimonial, which I waived by agreeing to leave. I'm one of only thirteen players to have won the Scottish Cup with the club, but it was like they tried to sneak me out the back door when I left.

A lot of players get to say their goodbyes to the supporters, but I was never allowed that opportunity. When I played for Dundee against United at the start of the 2006–07 season, I was worried about the kind of reaction I'd get from the United fans. Derby days are unforgiving, and the fans tend to give it tight to the opposition players, but the United supporters were great to me. As I ran off at the end of the warm-up, a wee girl called Levi, who always used to cheer for me, as I was her favourite Dundee United player, called me over. I ran to her and gave her a wee kiss. The United fans gave me a cheer and chanted my name. It must be the only time a player wearing a Dundee jersey has ever been saluted by their fiercest rivals. It was an important moment for me. It allowed me to finally reach closure with United.

14

CLAIRE — MOTHER TO THREE BOYS

I MET Claire at St Margaret Mary's Secondary School in Castlemilk. Am I allowed to say that our eyes met across a crowded classroom? We first got to know each other because we had a few mutual pals, and to begin with we were just friends, although we would have the occasional snog. We also saw other people at that time. There was no pressure and no commitment. I was always at Claire's door, but that was mainly to deliver the *Sunday Mail* and *Sunday Post* to her house, as I was her family's paper boy from the age of 13. It was a brilliant arrangement – Claire's parents, Gerry and Marie, would get their papers for nothing, and I'd get a couple of rolls 'n' sausage courtesy of the McFadden household.

My relationship with Claire developed, and after we'd both been out with different people on and off, we knew that we wanted to spend more serious time together. We were 16 at that time. I was delighted, because I had fancied Claire for ages, and I was the one who pushed for us to move things beyond friendship.

It wasn't long afterwards that I was thrust into the spotlight as part of the Scotland Under-16 World Cup team. People would stop me in the street and wish me all the best for the semi-final or the final. Claire would ask me who they were, and I'd have absolutely no idea. She couldn't get her head round my first brush with fame. She still can't. But that's football fans in Scotland for you: they love the game, and some can make a real fuss over players. But Claire has never been impressed with footballers. I've always just been Andrew to her. And always will be.

Our relationship became a long-distance one when I joined Dundee United in the summer of 1989. It wasn't perfect by any means, but it meant we both really looked forward to the weekends when I was allowed back to Glasgow. My first stop would be at Claire's to spend time with her, then I'd go to Mum's to drop off my bag of dirty washing.

The news that she was expecting a baby came as a real shock. But it was worse for her than it was for me. It wasn't the best of circumstances, but we were lucky to have good family and friends around us. They were all very supportive. Claire's mum, in particular, was brilliant – just different class. They all took the pressure away and made sure that everything was ready for Dylan's arrival: the pram; the cot. Everyone chipped in to make sure it would be as smooth as possible.

How Claire managed to cope with it all, I'll never know. I was hardly ever there, and I was probably of little use to her when I was. As time passed and my drinking got out of control, Claire left me many times, simply because she couldn't take any more. She had to pack her bags for the sake of her sanity. I drove her mad.

Apart from my drinking, I let her and our boys down far too often when it came to supporting them financially. Claire has never been one to go out and run riot with the credit cards and spoil herself with designer labels. It's not her thing – she's not extravagant in any way. All she wanted was for me to give her and the boys some attention – to spend some quality time with them. I believe that giving a person your time is worth more than anything.

However, Claire does like to make sure Dylan and Tyler are smartly turned out and have their fun. I can remember times when she'd get the boys ready to go into the town shopping and say to them that they'd get new trainers and then go for a McDonald's.

I'd tell her that there was plenty of money in the bank and that she could take out as much as she wanted. But I'd be lying. I'd know that there was nothing in the account. I might have been out on a bender and spent three or four hundred quid with guys I'd just met in a boozer, playing at Jack the Lad. Or I'd have bought cocaine or been down the bookies. It could have been any of a number of reasons, but it was mainly down to drink.

On these occasions, Claire's family used to bail us out. I can't remember the number of times her granny Wee Sadie and Auntie Margaret would dip into their purse to help us out. Mortgage payments, presents for the kids: God knows how much they gave us over the years. I've tried to pay them back as much as I can, but no matter how much I give them it will never be enough for the kindness they showed us.

I used to leave the house knowing that Claire only had a tenner in her purse and that she was going to the hole in the wall but there was nothing left in our account. I'd wasted the lot. The kids wouldn't get their shoes, far less a Happy Meal. I didn't have the courage to tell her to her face that I had spent the money. I just wanted to get out of the house and go to my game. Inevitably, the phone call would come an hour or two later, and I'd brace myself when her name flashed up on my mobile. Somehow, it didn't seem as bad when I was getting a blast down the phone.

On one occasion, Claire went shopping for a new pram and other things that we needed for the baby's arrival. She thought that I had close to £2,000 put away, but the two grand was a lie – I'd spent it. I just can't defend that kind of selfish behaviour. Sometimes she'd have no money for nappies, but I'd be out buying everybody a drink in the pub. I should never have treated her so badly, and my boys deserved better.

She could have turned her back on me and gained her revenge many times. But she never did. Even when I was coming off the drink and would wake up in the middle of the night, shaking uncontrollably, the bed soaking with sweat, she was the one who nursed me, held me down and told me that things would work out fine. I'd be scared to go back to sleep, because I'd think that I was going to fall off the bed. I'd be hallucinating, imagining that there were snakes on our bedroom floor. Claire would calm me down and rock me to sleep.

Claire has been a calming influence throughout my life but doesn't suffer this fool gladly. She's put me in my place and given me the 'hairdryer' treatment more times than I care to remember. In fact, she's given me bigger dressing-downs than most of the managers I've ever played under.

Whenever it got to the stage that I was just ignoring her, she'd tell me to pack my bags and show me the door. Sometimes, we'd be apart for months, and during those times I'm ashamed to admit that I went with other women. Claire's aware of my indiscretions. It's just another of my many failings that she has had to put up with over the years.

But it's not all been doom and gloom, and we've had many good times together. The day I think I made Claire most happy was when I proposed to her in 2002. It took weeks and weeks of planning. Mark Reilly helped me put it all together during our journeys to and from training at Rugby Park.

Mark Reilly: I travelled with Andy to training every day, and we formed a good relationship. We were open and could ask one another anything. After a few months, I kept on at him to propose to Claire. I told him she more than deserved to feel that special moment when the man she loved asked her to marry him.

Andy came into the car one morning and told me that he was going to go for it. He was going to ask Bobby Williamson for a Monday off so that he could take Claire away for a long weekend. I was delighted for him. He appeared to be so happy, and for the next wee while that was all he spoke about in the car.

To be fair, Andy was a bubbly character from the first day he joined Kilmarnock, and I'd say with certainty that there isn't a bad bone in his body. After all that he has been through in his life, he deserves credit for overcoming so many hurdles.

Because of his addictions and the choices he made during his career, people often say that Andy underachieved and wasted his talent. I prefer to look at it the other way and take the line that he has over-achieved. When you think he was drinking heavily and taking drugs for years and years, he should never have been able to play full-time football at Premier League level. Yet he battled his illness and bounced back to have a terrific career with Kilmarnock.

I'd played against him a few times when he was with Dundee United but didn't truly appreciate his talent as a footballer until we were in training every day and on the same side in matches. For me, Andy was the best crosser of a ball I've ever played with. His deliveries were inch-perfect – in the same class as David Beckham's.

He is also a courageous man, and credit to him for getting his life back together. On our way to training, we'd ask one another what we'd been up to the night before, and he'd always say that he'd been at his AA meeting. He was open and honest about his shortcomings as a person.

Claire had always wanted to visit Rome, so I booked us a weekend away and chose an engagement ring. I was nervous and knew I'd probably pick the wrong one, so I took Claire's sister Donna along for advice. I didn't want Claire to know the plan, so I plonked the ring inside a pair of my socks. But disaster struck when we landed in Italy. Our bags didn't turn up at the carousel, and we had to go to our hotel without any luggage.

We went out for a wee walk and some food, returning to our hotel later that night. Still no bags. The next morning, I wanted to see the Coliseum. It was a lovely day, and the sun was splitting the stones. On our way there, we stopped and watched as a wedding party passed us in the street. Claire asked me if I'd brought her to Rome to propose to her, and I told her that wasn't my intention

– it was just to get a wee break from the kids. There was another wedding down the road, and I thought, 'That's all I need.'

On our return to the hotel, the bag was waiting for us, so I checked inside my socks. The ring was still there, and it wasn't damaged. Brilliant. My plan could swing into action.

We went for dinner and then headed to the Trevi Fountain. Claire had always dreamed of going there, and I thought it was the perfect place to propose. I went down on one knee and asked her to marry me. She was ecstatic and accepted. She was absolutely beaming and started showing off the ring to the tourists who were beside us. She even got an Australian couple to take photos of us. So, the romantic side in me came out. And seeing Claire so happy made me feel absolutely elated.

With all the bad times we've had, it makes us appreciate the good days even more. But we're in no rush to get married. I know we will one day, because Claire is the only woman I ever want to spend serious time with. In the past, I've let her down far too often. But she knows me better than I know myself, and I can't hide anything from her. She's always been there for me, even though I've sometimes treated her like a dog. Whenever my back was against the wall, she was there. When I was on a downer, she was the one I wanted to be with. When I was in the Priory, she was the one who came to see me to make sure I was doing OK.

I often think that perhaps I ruined her life and that she could have been with another person who would have shown her the love, honesty and consideration she deserved. She has had terrible times, and most of them have been because of me. I'd turn to her for comfort, but I was never there for her when she was having a bad day. I never gave her a shoulder to cry on – never hugged her and told her she needn't worry.

At other times, she's been like a mum to me. I've often said that she's had three boys to bring up. She's had less trouble from Dylan and Tyler, though. She's a wonderful woman and a great mother, and she has been the most understanding and patient partner any man could ask for. She is my best pal. And I can say with absolute certainty that I would not be here today had it not been for her love and support. At best, I'd be on a park bench somewhere.

I've often asked her – and I know countless other people have, too – why she bothered to put up with me. Her answer to me was always simple: 'Because I love you, and deep down I know you are a good person.' Claire never detested me. It was my addiction she had no time for. She hated what alcohol did to me and hated it when I was taking drugs. She always said to me that when I was good, I was good. And when I was bad, I was bloody awful.

I'm just glad that since 2000 she has had, to an extent, the 'Andrew' she always wanted. I'm not perfect and never will be, but I can make Claire happy. And as long as she knows I'm putting the effort in, that will be good enough for her.

15

DYLAN AND TYLER —
MAKING UP FOR LOST TIME

IF I had the ability to turn back the clock, there are so many things I'd do differently and so many wrongs I'd love to put right. I've done so many stupid things in my life.

My two sons are the main reasons why I feel this way. They missed out on so much when they were younger, particularly Dylan, because of my drinking and selfish behaviour. I wasn't the dad I should have been. I'm trying to make up for lost time but realise I'm playing catch up with my kids.

When the end of the season arrived, players would have a nice holiday booked to go away with their families and spend some time in the sun having fun. Me? I never had anything sorted. I didn't look upon the six-week close-season break as the opportunity to spend quality time with my family. I regarded it as a chance for me to have a few good sessions whenever I felt like it. I could drink on a Friday night and get up and go straight to the pub on a Saturday at opening time. Magic.

It wasn't only during the summer that I put myself before them. It was pretty much all of the time. I'd come home drunk and be full of promises: 'Right, boys, Dad will take you swimming tomorrow. We'll get up, go to the baths and then go for a burger and a Coca-Cola.' The kids would be up first thing, rolling their trunks inside their towels, looking forward to a day at the swimming pool with their dad. They couldn't have been more excited if Santa had been coming with a sack full of presents. But I'd get out of bed and have no recollection of what I'd said to them the night before. I'd be rattling, choking for a drink. It came down to a choice: swimming with my boys or a few pints. No contest – the only thing getting wet that morning was my throat. I'd walk out the door and leave them in tears.

On the few occasions I did spend time with them, it was really because I felt I had to, not because I wanted to. Most of the time I'd rather have been in the company of a few beers. I'd go to the pictures with them and fall asleep, either because I was tired from the exertions of the previous night or because I'd drunk a few beers before going to the cinema.

However, I can honestly say that the happiest two weeks of my life came in the summer of 2001, and it was all down to spending time with my boys. We went on a family holiday to Florida. Claire's not keen on flying, but we decided to go for it. The four of us headed off to the States and had a ball. Life was good at that time. I'd been sober for 15 months, had just enjoyed a good season with Kilmarnock and had played for Scotland. I was also getting on great with Claire.

We stayed in a lovely hotel on International Drive, visited all the theme parks and had a great time at SeaWorld. I particularly remember one point when we were all sitting watching a dolphin show and I had Tyler on my knee. It was beautiful. The sun was shining and everybody was smiling. I just burst into tears. I became very emotional and couldn't control my feelings. Looking at my boys and how happy they were made me so overjoyed but also a little regretful that I hadn't enjoyed that kind of quality time a lot sooner. I had robbed them of so many smiles over the years, but I was now making up for it.

When I started to cry, I handed Tyler to Claire and went for a walk. I thought that I was going off my head, so I phoned one of the guys in AA to tell him how I was feeling. He said it was totally normal – a sure sign that I was getting better and the relationship with my family was on the up. I was pleased to hear him say that, as for long spells I had felt like an outsider when I was in the company of Claire and the boys. They had all been through so much together, and the boys would talk to her about anything. In Florida, I felt the love of my boys and was able to be a part of their lives. I didn't feel there were any barriers on that holiday. It was just perfect. I often look at the photos from that time, and they never fail to bring a smile to my face.

On our return, it was a case of trying to build on that holiday, and I feel, in many ways, I have. I've tried to make up for lost time and do things with them that I was not capable of doing, or refused to do, when I was drinking. At long last, I am being the dad I want to be and giving them the dad they truly deserve.

Dylan missed out the most. I wasn't there for the first four or five years of his life. Claire brought him up in Glasgow, and I stayed in Dundee to play football. I wish I was able to have played a bigger part in his life at that stage. Dylan probably feels he never had a dad. I'll never stop feeling regret about that.

He's a teenager now and knows I'm there for him. In the past few years, we've shared so many good times. I've tried to take him to as many football games as possible, and we've had memorable occasions going to watch Celtic during their fantastic run to the UEFA Cup final in 2003 and in their Champions League campaigns.

When we've had time together, I've warned him about the dangers of alcohol and what else that can lead to. Don't get me wrong, I want him to be able to enjoy a pint as much as the next guy, but I'd hate to see him make the same mistakes I did. That would tear me apart. As part of his education, I've taken him along to AA meetings to let him see what it's about for me and why I need to attend. It's also to give him knowledge and understanding of what life is all about and see the efforts I'm making to make sure I never go off the rails again.

Yet for all the problems I've faced in my life, it was Dylan who came closest to dying. In December 2006, he was attacked on the street in Castlemilk. It was a Friday night at about 11 p.m. and he was out with his pals. It was a random attack. A few boys jumped him and plunged a bottle into his face and neck. He made his way to his gran's, and I got a phone call to go and pick him up. We took him to the Victoria Infirmary, but he was quickly moved to the Southern General Hospital for specialist treatment. The medical staff, Claire and I spent hours picking pieces of glass out of his face, and his neck wouldn't stop bleeding.

Dylan asked me if he was going to die. I reassured him and told him he was going to be fine, but I wasn't convinced. I left his bedside, went to the toilet and started to sob uncontrollably.

We were in the hospital until 10.30 the following night, and I was just glad to be there for him. We never left his side, because he needed constant reassurance. It made me realise how vulnerable your children can be and how vital the role of parent is. It's the most important job in the world and the most difficult. The circumstances weren't ideal, but a positive to come out of Dylan being hospitalised was that I felt a strong bond with him. It made me realise how much I loved him and reinforced just how much my children mean to me. It's about getting my priorities right.

Dylan was in hospital for a few days and was treated excellently by the medical staff. But the attack has had a negative effect on him, no doubt about it. It's been a major setback, and his confidence has been severely dented. We just hope that time will be a healer, in terms of his self-assurance and also for the scars to heal. Claire massages cream into his face and neck every night. We're sure the marks will clear up in time.

Tyler was also worried about Dylan's health, and he was so

pleased when his brother pulled through. Like all brothers, they have their 'moments', but Tyler was visibly upset at what happened to Dylan.

Tyler is totally different to his older brother. He is a quiet, sensitive lad, who loves singing and dancing, and he enjoys drama classes and participating in school plays. He's also tidier, and you can leave him to clean up a mess. I wish his brother was the same.

Tyler's not interested in football, and in many ways that's been a good thing. I wouldn't want to subject him to the verbal abuse I receive at almost every ground in the country. It's horrible to hear opposition fans calling me a fucking junkie and an alky. Dylan has sampled it, and he didn't like it.

The nearest Tyler gets to seeing his dad playing football is when we have a game on the PlayStation. He has a competitive streak and does not like losing. Dylan is the same. They both get that from me. They both skelp me at football, which does not go down well at all, so we've stopped playing that and have switched to the Tiger Woods golf game. I can win at that. Now, though, they refuse to play me at golf because they can't get the better of me!

Overall, I'm so proud of my sons. And I hope they are proud of me, despite the many occasions I've let them down. I hope to be able to spend more time with them in the future and look forward to the day when they have kids of their own and make me a grandfather. I suppose that would give me the chance to try to make up for the mistakes I made, particularly with Dylan. That would mean so much to me.

For as much as I would give anything in this world to be able to start afresh and wipe out my neglect, I can't change the past and can't continue to beat myself up over my appalling behaviour when I was on drink and drugs. I have the chance to make sure the future's good for them, thank God, and that will always give me a reason to get out of bed in the morning. Claire has lots of good memories from being with them, and I'm now in the process of building a nice memory bank of my own, which is fantastic, because my sons mean everything to me. It feels good to be a loving father to them. It feels really good.

16

BACK ON THE BOOS

I REALLY didn't fancy moving down to the Second Division to play on a permanent basis, but Morton were ambitious, many of the players were talented, the dressing-room was lively and Jim McInally treated me like an adult. He was able to persuade me that the Greenock club were my best option and that I would be a big part of his plans.

The two-year contract was structured as a one-year deal with the option of another year if I played in more than twenty games. I knew I'd pass that milestone no problem. In fact, I had visions of ending my career at Morton. I could genuinely see myself staying there for four or five years and helping the club climb the divisions all the way to the SPL. Morton are a big club with a huge fan base in Inverclyde. I could see the potential and hoped to be part of a new era.

When I was at Cappielow on loan, we just failed to win promotion, and we missed out again in my first full season, Gretna romping away with the title. However, we had a really good season, and under normal circumstances our points total would have been enough to take us up. Instead, we were in the play-offs, and we lost out to Peterhead. I was angry at not winning promotion and frustrated with myself, as I felt my form had dipped towards the end of the season. Being abused as a child was preying on my mind at that point, and I decided to open up to McInally about it and confide in him.

The chat took place at the training ground, and his assistant manager Martin Clark was also there. It was quite informal, and I felt totally at ease speaking to them, as we had always enjoyed a good relationship. They seemed sympathetic to my situation and even put me in touch with someone who eventually led me to Angela Maguire. I left the meeting feeling good at having got things off my chest and looked forward to a rest during the summer and getting my complete focus back.

A few days later, I received a phone call from one of my teammates. He told me that he'd heard a rumour I was leaving Morton. I told him that the rumour was rubbish. I had no inclination to go and had never been given the impression that Jim wanted shot of me.

However, a couple of days later I found out that the lad was spot on. I was playing golf with Derek McInnes when my mobile went off. It was McInally. There was no time for small talk: 'Hi, Andy. Listen, we're letting you go. We think it's time for you to move on.'

'What do you mean?'

'It's just time for a parting of the ways, and I'm not going to change my mind.'

I reminded Jim that the clause in my contract had kicked in and I still had a year of my contract to go. I let him know that I didn't want to leave, but if I wasn't going to be part of his plans then I should be compensated. I was on a basic wage of £650 a week at Morton, so I was due more than £30,000. I told Jim that if he thought I was going to give him problems during the new season, then that was up to him, but, obviously, I'd need to be compensated for my contract being terminated early. When I mentioned money, Jim's reply was, 'Don't go down that road, Andy.' End of conversation.

I was in a state of shock. I told Derek, who had played for

Morton, what had happened, and he told me to go home, phone the SPFA and seek some legal advice. My mind was in overdrive trying to work out where this bombshell had come from. I'd had no disciplinary problems at Morton, and I had played well for them that season. I also got on well with the management.

I cast my mind back to the meeting we'd had a few days earlier, and the only thing I could think of was that they were frightened of the fact I had been on Valium for a short period of time during my second spell at Dundee United. As I mentioned before, I went through a rough patch there and was prescribed the drug to help me cope. United boss Ian McCall knew about it, and it was all above board. In fact, McCall gave me time off to help my recovery. I hadn't been taking any medication while I was at Morton, but maybe they were scared that there could be some sort of drugs scandal and they would be seen in a bad light. I'm really not sure. Looking back on it now, I believe that if I hadn't mentioned Valium, everything would have been fine, and I would probably still be playing for them now.

Morton released the news of my departure to the media and made out it was because I wanted to play at a higher level. Utter garbage. Morton handled the whole situation in a very cold manner. I never deserved to be treated that way. Not only did they fail to honour the final year of my deal, but they also stopped my wages from that moment onwards. They never paid me another penny. I was due money all through the summer and for the rest of the new season, so why would I agree to walk away when I had nothing else lined up?

I phoned the SPFA to ask for advice and assistance. I wanted their legal team involved, but they insisted that we keep it within the parameters of the game. They looked at a copy of my contract and agreed that Morton had no right to bin me. It was there in black and white that it had one more year to run. We wrote a letter to the SFL to ask for a hearing, but, to the best of my knowledge, we never heard back from them, even though I personally delivered the letter to the SFL offices at Hampden.

As far as I'm concerned, I'm still owed in excess of £30,000 from Morton. I know it's more than a year since we parted, but that's irrelevant. Even if it was ten years ago, they still owe me that sum, because I never signed a release form.

Right now, I have no idea where things stand. I made several attempts to keep in touch with the SPFA for updates, but it appeared to be a one-way street. I've no idea if they are still fighting my case or if they stuck my file in an old cardboard box in a broom cupboard. However, I intend to look into it all again, and I won't give up the fight to reclaim what's rightfully mine.

That said, I was genuinely pleased when Morton won promotion to the First Division at the end of the 2006–07 season. I'm still in touch with a few of the lads, and it was great to see their hard work being rewarded. It was also payback time for the Morton fans. They are a loyal bunch, and I played in front of 6,000 in some games. After missing out on promotion on a few occasions in recent years, it must have been a great feeling for them to finally get that monkey off their back. It also put to bed the ridiculous claims that there was a betting scam at the club. Two seasons before I'd arrived, it had been alleged that some of the Morton players had bet on their own team to lose and that they'd thrown away promotion. For what's it worth, players do like to do a fixed-odds coupon, but they never bet against themselves, especially when they have a chance of winning promotion.

Morton can go from strength to strength and do have the potential to be an SPL club, no doubt about it. Greenock is a passionate footballing area, and if they can bring in some extra revenue, they will always be able to attract decent quality to the club. I know I'd rather see Morton in the SPL instead of a club like Gretna, and I mean that with all due respect to Brooks Mileson and his players.

Having my wages stopped by Morton meant another summer

without any income. Of course, the same thing had happened during the 2003 close season when I had turned down a new deal from Kilmarnock to try and win a contract with Hibs. Admittedly, back then, I had been at fault. But not this time. On this one, I was blameless. And it's not often I've been able to say that.

It was a tough spell wondering where my next wage packet was coming from. But out of the blue, I received a phone call from Alex Rae. Alex had just taken over as manager of Dundee and wanted experienced players to help him push for promotion to the SPL. I met Alex in Glasgow, and he outlined his plans. I was impressed with his vision. The journey back and forward to Dundee didn't appeal, but the prospect of playing regular football did, especially in a higher division than Morton. I also knew from my 11 years at Dundee United just how big a club Dundee were, and I wanted to help them realise their potential once again.

Before I signed a contract, I phoned the SPFA to find out where I stood legally with my complaint against Morton. Fraser assured me that it would not harm my case to join a new club. I was free to earn a living elsewhere, as well as pursue Morton for their breach of contract.

I knew some Dundee fans would have concerns about me coming to play for them, but I also knew I was good enough to win them over, and I scored on my debut – a pre-season friendly away to Forfar. I then injured my calf in another pre-season game, away to Arbroath, and that ruled me out for the first month of the season.

In my first match back, we defeated Gretna 4–0 away from home, and I was delighted to score a goal. It should have been a springboard for us, but we had quite a young team, and we were just too inconsistent, which, to be fair, was typical of many teams in that division. Gretna won promotion to the SPL. Their experienced players managed to get them over the winning line on the last day of the season after they had been put under serious pressure by St Johnstone.

I had fun at Dundee. Quite a number of players travelled from the west of Scotland up to Tayside, and Ludovic Roy and I pestered the chief executive Dave McKinnon to let us use one of the club's minibuses to commute in. We told him it would be good for team spirit and would also save a few of the boys a small fortune in petrol money! Davie agreed and there were between seven and ten of us on the bus on any given day. I was a complete and utter pest, if truth be told. Some of the boys would want a kip on the way to training, others wanted some peace and quiet on the way back down the road. I never let them get either. I'd turn the music up full blast or bore them stiff with my patter. A few attempts were made to throw me off, but I always managed to withstand their efforts.

It may have been a laugh off the pitch, but on it our results weren't going too well. In lower-division games, you can hear every word of abuse belted out at you, and you can usually pinpoint the people involved. I used to take pelters from opposition fans. On my debut for Morton away to Stranraer, I was punched on the back of the head by a Blues supporter as I prepared to take a throw-in. The fans just laughed at me. I looked towards the police for help. They laughed too. I felt humiliated.

Partick Thistle fans complained to the police about me after a game at Firhill when I was with Dundee. The Jags fans chanted, 'Andy, Andy, what's the score?' and I gave them a two-fingered salute. Well, we were 2–0 down, so I gave them the perfect response to their question. The fans couldn't wait to report me, and the police match commander had a word with me at the end of the game.

I found it really difficult not being able to respond when I was being called a junkie bastard or an alky. I'd sometimes hit back with some choice words of my own, and people would be off again to the police demanding my arrest.

I can take a bit of banter at football games and don't mind too much when I get a bit of a slagging. Some of it is quite amusing, and the patter has made me laugh out loud a few times. But when it starts to get really personal and makes reference to my past involvement with drink and drugs, it can affect me. You know, if the fans were calling me a 'black bastard', a 'Fenian bastard' or an 'orange bastard', they'd be under the microscope, and there would be pressure on their respective clubs to ban them or the police to charge them. But it's perfectly acceptable for them to have a pop at my illness. And some members of the police force have laughed at the comments made.

When these grown men chant their bile at me, they've no idea the impact it has. I'd like to think the football authorities and the police would look at this issue and address it. I don't believe it's right that only black players and players from the Old Firm are protected from some of the morons who attend football games.

My own behaviour was brought into question when I played for Dundee in a game against Clyde at Broadwood in December 2006. I was given three red cards by referee Dougie McDonald. I'm not saying that I was completely innocent, but, frankly, the ref was a disgrace that day. He treated me like some sort of school kid, and I felt as though he was looking down his nose at me. He made a mountain out of a molehill. Some of my actions were wrong, and I freely admit that, but to be sent off three times was a joke.

It all started when Gavin Swankie scored a penalty for us and I tried to retrieve the ball. There was five minutes left and we were 2–0 down, but the goal brought us back into the game. I wrestled for the ball with Clyde goalie Davie Hutton, and I received a yellow card. I gave the ref a bit of verbal for cautioning me. He then produced a second yellow for my backchat and I was given my marching orders. I couldn't believe it. I lost the plot and told him he was a fucking joke. I then received another red for that outburst. As I ran off, I was confronted by Eddie Malone of Clyde, and he told me to 'get off the pitch, ya fucking prick'. I pushed him in the face, although it was wrongly claimed that I punched him.

I was back in the dressing-room when John Boggan, one of our subs that day, came in and told me that the ref wanted me to go back out so that he could give me a third red for the Malone incident. I refused to go. 'Fuck McDonald,' I thought. John was sent in again, but by this time I was undressed and only had a towel for support. I was fuming but decided to go out, if only to allow the game to restart. I was stopped halfway down the tunnel by a policeman who told me I could not go on the pitch dressed like that.

McDonald called me to his room after the game and told me that I'd be receiving a fourth red card for refusing to return to the field of play. I told him that was ridiculous and I would appeal. McDonald never included the fourth red in his match report. I later received an eight-game ban from the SFA.

When I look back, it was much ado about nothing. It wasn't as though I'd been involved in an Eric Cantona-style incident. It was really all because of an insipid little man with a whistle and the power to mess with players' livelihoods. Malone even sent a letter to the Dundee board to tell them that the third red card was totally unjustified.

On another day, I might not have shouted back at McDonald or have become involved with Malone. But frustration had been building up in me for a few weeks. I was playing beside too many kids at Dundee, and I felt the onus was on me to win games on my own, although I was never put under that kind of pressure by Alex or his assistant Davie Farrell. Maybe I tried too hard – tried to do too much to compensate for the lack of experience on the pitch.

That must have played a part in my loss of discipline, as I'd only ever been sent off twice in 14 years prior to that, so it wasn't as though I had a history of red cards or bad behaviour. Also, just a couple of weeks before, Dylan had been in hospital fighting for his life after he had been attacked in the street. But most referees never take anything like that into account. You sometimes wonder if there is an ounce of compassion in them. I certainly wondered that about McDonald.

It's just typical of refs in the modern game. I hate to sound like some old pro harping on about the good old days, but early in my career you could have a chat with the ref. A bit of banter was part and parcel of the game. The ref took it, but he dished it out too, and players always knew how far they could take it. It's a cliché, but football's a man's game and men do swear. There are refs in charge of games now who will pull you up for any form of expletive. It's petty shite.

Dundee didn't take kindly to the eight-game ban, and I heard on the radio that they planned to sack me. I'm not the kind of guy to hang about somewhere I'm not wanted – I'd already had my fingers burned a few months earlier at Morton – so I agreed to a pay-off of one month's salary, even though I had more than six months of my deal to run.

Alex Rae: I was delighted to get Andy to Dundee. I knew he was a talented footballer and would bring some vital experience to the dressing-room and be a real asset on the park. It was a blow when he got injured in pre-season. In fact, we lost three other players who would have started every game for me, and to be without them for the best part of a month crippled us. Results weren't what we hoped for, and it took a while for our season to get going.

During his time at Dens Park, Andy made a good contribution and scored one of the goals of the season – a brilliant effort against Queen of the South. I think he let himself down in his final game against Clyde, but there was a lot of pressure on him at that time after what had happened to his son Dylan. However, he wasn't the only guilty party that day.

There's no doubt that he was a target for opposing players, and he took severe personal verbal abuse from the opposition fans. I used to get it as well, and I always tried to take it as a compliment. Fans only slaughter you if they see you as a danger to their side collecting a victory. Sometimes, though, Andy let it all get to him. That was a pity, because he was at his happiest when he was playing football. He could leave any worries behind, and when he was fully concentrated there were few better than him. Playing football fulfils a lot of needs, mentally and physically, and I hope Andy can have as many years playing football as he wants. I was glad when he got fixed up with Ayr United after his spell with Dundee came to an end.

There's no doubt it saddened me how it ended for him at Dundee. We missed him. He was such a good influence in the dressing-room, and the lads looked up to him. But Andy has it in him to bounce back from disappointments, and he will believe that he still has a positive contribution to make to the Scottish game.

After the Dundee debacle, I thought seriously about quitting football. I reckoned that there was little point busting my backside when it felt as though I was going to be a marked man by referees and officials. In the lower divisions, I seemed to be constantly in trouble with refs, opposition fans and the police. I was fed up. I only wanted to continue playing if I could get back to the SPL or down south again.

Since admitting to my alcohol problem, I've relied on the support of friends and professional people to help me through the problems in my life. This was another traumatic time, and Peter Kay of Tony Adams' Sporting Chance Clinic was particularly supportive. He invited me to his clinic in London for five days of therapy. It was great to go there and get away from all the crap up in Scotland. Footballers such as Adrian Mutu, Joey Barton and Fernando Ricksen have all attended Peter's clinic. I enjoyed it there. I spent time with people with all sorts of problems, and being able to talk about my own issues brought a great deal of comfort. When I left the clinic, I was back in a 'good zone'.

Peter Kay: We provide counselling, treatment and aftercare for people with lifestyle problems, such as gambling or alcohol. The English PFA are a major sponsor of ours, and we have a link to the SPL. I've met Andy a few times, and it is not a weakness to ask for help. Andy has shown tremendous strength of character to address his problems over the years. He was frustrated at letting himself down after the incident at Broadwood and came to me. It was great to be in his company. He is an honest man and full of integrity.

Dr Ian McGuinness was also a wonderful help to me. He worked with Rangers for a few years and has great people skills. He was a welcome sounding board.

In January 2007, I got in touch with my old gaffer Jim Jefferies to see if he would offer me training facilities at Kilmarnock to keep me ticking over until I was able to play again. Being unable to play any football for eight games was not pleasant, and it meant I'd be on the sidelines until early February 2007.

I've so much respect for Jim Jefferies and Billy Brown, and I hoped they would offer me a deal. Sadly, they didn't. However, word was out that I was training with them, and a few managers got in touch to ask Billy and Jim about my situation. They gave positive feedback.

My only disappointment at that time was that no SPL club offered me a deal. But I had many offers – about seven in total – and the one that appealed to me most was Ayr United. Robert Connor and Robert Reilly were in charge at United. I met Robert Reilly – who I used to watch when I was a kid and he was a star in the Clyde team – at a café in Glasgow, and we discussed a few things. Ayr had a chance of winning promotion that season, and I was up for the challenge of coming in and helping them out for the final nine games of the season. I signed for the club when I still had three games of my suspension to run.

On my first visit to Somerset Park as an Ayr player, I was booed by many of the home fans. Because of my connection to their fierce rivals Kilmarnock, a few of them even told me to get to fuck. Welcome to Ayr!

I knew the only way to get the fans on my side was to score goals and help the team win. I was confident I'd be able to achieve that. However, before I'd even kicked a ball for them, the two Roberts were sacked. We'd gone from promotion hopefuls to relegation contenders in the space of just a couple of weeks. I felt so sorry for them. I'd wanted to do my bit and repay their faith in me.

Brian Reid and Mark McGeown were asked to take over on a temporary basis. Both were still playing at the time but were happy to take on the extra responsibility. Their first game was away to Stranraer, and it was also my debut for Ayr. Stranraer were right in the relegation dogfight, and we had to beat them to keep a safe distance between us. We won the game, and I scored. There was no problem with the Ayr fans now. Suddenly, they wanted to meet me and shake my hand.

Big Reidy continued to achieve decent results, but the Ayr board wanted a more experienced man to take over, which was understandable. However, I know Reidy would have made a good go of it if he'd been given the opportunity.

Neil Watt was the man the Ayr directors identified, and he came in to take over with a few games of the season remaining. By that stage, we were out of the danger zone but had no chance of going up. I played nine games for Ayr, and we only lost once. I felt good in that division and just wished that I'd had the chance to come in earlier to make an impact, but my suspension had put paid to that.

I was immediately impressed with the new gaffer. He'd won promotion with Stranraer a few years earlier and knew what was required to get a club going and build good team spirit.

Neil doesn't need football. He is an extremely successful businessman, and there are no financial incentives for him to manage a part-time club. But he loves to win and likes to see his players and fans happy. He'll make a right good go of it at Ayr, and he will feel that he can repeat the success he had at Stranraer. The way he has treated me on and off the pitch has been absolutely superb. I have opened up to him about every problem I have encountered in my life, and he has shown nothing but support. One thing I know for sure – he's not the type of man to renege on a contract. His man-management skills are fantastic, and I want to give him that extra 10 per cent. He also has a very trustworthy assistant in Stuart Millar.

I genuinely hope Neil gets the chance to take us into the First Division, and then it will be up to the club to decide what to do after that. Do they stay part time and just hope to avoid relegation? Or do they go for it and try to move into the SPL within three years? I hope they decide to give it a go. But I don't want to look too far ahead. I, more than most, know that you can never look too far ahead in life, and it is a case of taking it a game at a time. I just hope I'm around, enjoying my football and playing my part in a success story at Ayr United. My contract runs until the end of the 2007–08 season, and we'll see what happens. As long as Neil is at the club, I will gladly be a part of it.

17

MY GAFFERS

WHEN I look back on my career, I realise that I've been fortunate to have played under so many good managers. Jim McLean will never be my favourite person, and I know for sure that I'll never feature in any great recollections of his career, but I have complete respect for his ability as a coach and the way he improved my game.

My earliest memory of McLean was when I was an S Form signing with Dundee United and he used to travel down to Glasgow at least once a week to cast his eye over United's west of Scotland signings. He got to know the boys, introduced himself and always remembered your name every time he came down. I don't imagine many managers would go to those lengths to ensure the talent coming through was up to the standard he demanded. But it just showed how dedicated and committed he was. Jim McLean was an obsessive – totally addicted to football.

I worked my way through the ranks at United and started working closely with McLean by the time I was 17. His training was different class, and he would regularly stop sessions to point something out or tell us where we were going wrong. Some managers stop training in the middle of a game just for the sake of it, but Jim always had a purpose and his point was usually right on the money. You always emerged from that 30-second stoppage a wiser player. He pulled me aside once to tell me that my body shape was all wrong when I was trying to turn a defender. He told me that my body opened up to the advantage of the opponent and that I had to do it differently. I worked on it and eventually cracked it. That was the great thing about United – they cared about the young players and tried hard to educate and improve them.

Jim used to run the bollocks off us at pre-season training. Looking back on it, the amount of running he made us do was unbelievable. Ridiculous, in fact. We'd do four seven-minute runs, then thirty-six hill runs up a sixty-yard climb. It was the old-fashioned run-until-you-drop-or-throw-up method. Some of the boys would collapse in a heap. Others would be sick. A lot of the lads would just hold their hands up and chuck it. I was lucky, as I was reasonably fit and could handle it. While others were close to tears, I would be laughing.

We rarely had a day off during my first two or three years at Tannadice, and we were always back out in the afternoons doing extra work on our games. I don't believe young players do enough of that now. Too many are out the door to do something else as soon as their morning session is over.

Jim's training was always different and never repetitive. It was always geared towards the game on the Saturday, and we'd study the strengths and weaknesses of our opponents as the week wore on.

Wee Jim was also really superstitious, and he'd religiously stick to the same routine if it had been successful in the past. Personally, I've never gone in for all of that stuff. Does putting your right boot on before your left boot or running out of the tunnel seventh in the line-up or sitting on a certain seat on the team bus make you play better? No, I don't think so. However, I respect boys that go in for that kind of thing. From memory, Paul Sturrock, Maurice Malpas and Steven Pressley were superstitious at United.

Jim would take it to extremes, though. He'd play boys at certain away grounds if they had played well there in the past. If we won one week with a certain kit on, he'd insist that we wore the same strips the following week – washed of course! If we were playing at Ibrox or Parkhead, he'd make sure that we stayed in the same hotel if we'd had a good result while staying there on the previous occasion. We'd stay in the Westerwood at Cumbernauld, but if we lost we'd move to a hotel in Moodiesburn the next time. We had to travel by the same route and have the same bus driver as well. And Jim would have the same meal to eat before the match. If we lost, we'd go a different route – even if it meant adding half an hour onto the journey.

I was quite a confident footballer, but Jim gave me extra belief in myself. I never feared any defender. If I was on my game, I was sure that I'd get the better of any man-marker. That said, when David Robertson played at left-back for Rangers, I always found him to be particularly difficult to play against, because he always loved to bomb forward and I had to track back to help with the defensive duties. As he got older, it wasn't such a problem, as David would struggle to get back into his own half, and I would still be full of energy as I ran past him. Playing against Tosh McKinlay was also a shift and a half. Tosh loved going forward when he played for Hearts and Celtic, and I never enjoyed that aspect of my game against him. But I'm sure Tosh would have a few rough memories of me, too.

The most important thing Jim taught me was to get the ball in the box. 'Put it into a dangerous area and give the opposition something to think about,' he'd say. 'Make them work.' In my early days, I thought that I always had to beat my opponent before sending the ball over. Garbage. It makes no difference whether you deliver a cross in line with the penalty spot or from the chalk on the dead-ball line – it's about the area you send it to. David Beckham has hardly beaten a full-back in his life, but he must have had hundreds and hundreds of assists because of the quality of the ball he delivers. Jim introduced that into my game.

However, for all I enjoyed working with Jim when we had the balls out, I thought that his man management was dreadful. Shocking, in fact. He would fine us for trivial shite, and I could never condone his methods on that front. He reduced many of the boys to tears. Some of the lads even nicknamed him 'Ayatollah' because of the hard-line approach he took to management.

McLean had an excellent reputation as a football man, but in the final four or five years of his reign at United more and more horror stories spread around the game about the scandalous way he treated players – so much so that some Scottish players would point-blank refuse to sign for United, as they just didn't want to work with him. That's why he had to dive into the foreign market and bring over players who knew nothing about his reputation. Sadly, a lot of the players he brought over were poor quality and nowhere near the standard of British footballers. He signed two Argentinian lads. The first of them, Walter Rojas, signed in 1991, must go down as one of United's worst-ever signings. He cost £200,000 but never kicked a ball for the first team. The other was a guy called Victor Ferreyra.

The South American boys used to drive wee Jim nuts. When he wanted to make a point to them about what they were doing wrong, they pretended not to understand English. Of course, when it came to discussions about bonus money, they could speak the lingo no problem.

Jim also insisted players stay in and around Dundee and wouldn't let players commute from more than 25 miles away in Perth. Again, that put players off. And when I think back to some of the screaming matches at half-time (the hairdryer treatment from Sir Alex Ferguson couldn't have been as bad), it still makes me shudder. At the interval, I used to pray that he wasn't going to let rip at me, even if I had played well in the first 45 minutes. If he started off shouting at someone else, I'd hope that they would answer him back, as it would guarantee that he was kept busy for the whole 15 minutes! I'd be off the hook.

I remember one game when he was ranting and raving as usual at one of the boys at half-time. He was really angry and kicked out at a wastebasket in disgust. The trouble was, his foot got stuck in it. So, he hopped about the dressing-room as if nothing was wrong and continued to shout and bawl with a bin attached to his foot! I thought it would have been better for him to sit down, compose himself and pull his foot out. The boys were pissing themselves laughing – with their heads down, of course. Stuart Hogg, the fitness coach, was on the floor trying to pull the basket away from Jim's foot. It was comical. Honestly, what a sight.

Jim had no time for a player defending his own corner. He hated someone trying to reason with him. It was his way and only his way. There was no in between. I used to be terrified when he was having a go at me, but towards the end of my time at United I just found the whole thing silly and amusing. I never let it get to me. I had no fear of him at that point.

But I still respect the man and will never forget what he taught me. And his contribution to United will never be forgotten. Having won the Premier League in 1983, an unbelievable accomplishment, and taken the club to the UEFA Cup final in 1987, he is the most successful manager the club has ever had, and his achievements will never be surpassed.

Before I worked under Jim, Paul Sturrock was my manager at United. Paul was in charge of the youth and reserve set-ups. There's no doubt that I did not appreciate how good he was until I left. He gave me an excellent grounding to build my professional career on. Luggy was a world-class striker in his playing days, and he was especially good at coaching the front men. I benefited greatly from his experience and knowledge of the game. He'd take me for extra sessions, and a lot of the time he'd just walk me through things on the training pitch, teaching me how to play my position. It was nice and relaxed, and he always put his point across well.

Undoubtedly, there was pressure on him to promote players on to wee Jim for the first team. Credit to Paul for supplying player after player. He has played a part in a lot of careers, and United have so much to thank him for. Not just for his service as a player, but also for the way he improved the kids.

I was on YTS duties when I first went to Tannadice. I'd have to clean the first-team players' boots, tidy the dressing-room, prepare the kit for training, stuff like that. After Paul had checked we had completed our cleaning duties, he'd sit in the home dressing-room with us on a Friday afternoon and tell us how brilliant he was! His stories were good and so was his patter. Mind you, he had an awful taste in clobber.

Ivan Golac succeeded Jim McLean as manager, and his taste in clothes wasn't much better. But coming from Eastern Europe, he had a decent excuse. Ivan was the most confident manager I've ever worked under. He loved training with the boys, and his confidence worked its way through the whole squad. He had us believing we could beat any team in the land.

Some of his interviews in the papers were outrageous. Goodness, I remember him rating Jerren Nixon at £12 million after the guy played a few good games on the wing for us. Mind you, after the press had to deal with wee Jim for so long, it must have been refreshing for them to have a laid-back customer like Ivan with his rent-a-quote attitude.

In training, he loved the shooting drills and was different class at finishing. If you asked Ivan to stick the ball in the top-right or the bottom-left corner, he'd do it without a problem.

He managed us to Scottish Cup success in 1994 and played a huge role in our cup run. He gave us the belief to get through some tough ties en route to the final against Rangers. They were an outstanding team at that time, yet we beat them. Looking back, it was all down to Golac. He just had something about him that was perfect during that cup run. His team talks were never complicated. It was simple stuff, and a lot of his success was down to very good man management rather than great tactical know-how.

He was a bit of a character, and he loved to put us up in real fancy-dan hotels. We'd never complain, of course, but I'm sure the Tannadice accountant was in a sweat every other Monday when the bill came in from another five-star hotel that we'd stayed in at the weekend. Ivan liked the good life. On one occasion, we stayed at Cameron House on the banks of Loch Lomond for an away game at Kilmarnock. Ivan was in his element, mixing with the great and the good in the hotel.

He lost his job less than a year after our cup win, as we struggled in the league. I suppose his dismissal was to be expected. He couldn't live up to the achievement of our cup success, and it was always going to be downhill after that. But he can't have his achievements taken away from him. He'll always be regarded as a Dundee United legend, and he fully deserves that honour.

I had arguments with Golac, but I was still sorry to see him leave. Billy Kirkwood replaced him, but he couldn't keep us up that season. We were relegated to the First Division in May 1995. Going down came as a bit of a shock to us all. We never really seemed in any danger until we lost 2–0 away to Aberdeen with a few games to go, and that put us right in the relegation mix.

During the final couple of months of the season, we just couldn't get out of the slump we found ourselves in. Billy couldn't be directly blamed for that. And rather than being depressed when we went down, he and the club got their act together and decided that the only way to get out of the First Division at the first attempt was to act like a Premier League club. So, they didn't sell off all of the assets and instead brought in Steven Pressley, Ally Maxwell and Owen Coyle.

I never really appreciated just how badly affected the United fans were when we got relegated, because I moved back down to Glasgow for the summer. However, when we started to go to places like Dumbarton and Clydebank for league games, I knew exactly what we'd let happen. It wasn't pretty, and the only way to fix it was to go straight back up.

We sold Billy McKinlay to Blackburn Rovers for around £1.5

million, and that was a decent piece of business. He played the first few games of the season in the First Division, but you could tell it was hard for him to adjust. It was the same for Maurice Malpas – it must have been torture for him after so many years at the top with United and Scotland.

Kirkwood kept our spirits up and was excellent at making sure the dressing-room didn't get downhearted. He was upbeat and told us that we only had a few months to wait before we'd be back in with the big boys again. We did make it up, via the play-offs, but Billy didn't last long the following season and was sacked after a poor start to the campaign. I felt for Kirkie. He had played under Jim during the golden era, and there was too much pressure on him to revive the club from top to bottom. It couldn't have been easy for him with Jim constantly breathing over his shoulder.

Jim McLean was the chairman at that time, and he appointed his brother Tommy as the new manager. I was surprised to see Tommy take the job, but I suppose it told me that he was able to stand up to his brother and take no nonsense. From my position in the dressing-room, that appeared to be the case. There was respect between the two, and Tommy gave his brother his place, but he wouldn't let him cross the line.

When Tommy took over, we were bottom of the table but managed to finish the 1996–97 season third in the Premier League. It was a brilliant achievement, and if you take the Old Firm out of the equation, it meant that we won the league within the league. We also reached the Coca-Cola Cup final but lost out to Celtic at Ibrox.

Training was always bright under Tommy, and I enjoyed working with him. He may have had a slightly dour image, but he had a good sense of humour and was really approachable. I sat with him a few times in the dressing-room after training and had a blether about playing on the wing. Tommy was a top-class wide player in his day and played in the Rangers side that won the European

Cup-Winners' Cup in 1972 after defeating Moscow Dynamo in Barcelona. But I'd wind him up that there was much greater pressure on contemporary wingers to deliver a better-quality ball than there was in his era. I said that all he had to do was get plenty of height on his crosses and hope for the best, whereas I had to whip the ball in right onto the head of the striker. It was all good fun and showed he could take a bit of banter.

I think Tommy had a soft spot for me and wanted to see me make the most of my career. He was big on stats, and I remember he came into the dressing-room for one of our wee chats and told me that I had set up 16 of the 20 goals we'd scored so far that season. Robbie Winters and Kjell Olofsson were the strikers benefiting from my work, and they were a joy to play with. Robbie had wonderful speed and could leave defenders trailing by five or six yards over a twenty-yard run. If he had only possessed a wee bit more composure in front of goal, he would have played at the very highest level and won many more caps for Scotland. Kjell was brought in by Tommy and was a great signing. He worked hard and was a model professional. I was sorry to see Tommy leave United in September 1998.

I was equally sorry to let Tommy Burns down so badly when he was my gaffer at Reading. He tried to help me sort out my drinking, but it was a waste of time. Tommy was a manager who put his players first. He was passionate and worked round the clock to make a success of it at Reading. It never worked out for him, which was a pity, as he deserved to win promotion back to the old English First Division.

When Tommy left Reading, Alan Pardew took over. I was a lost cause by then, so I didn't get the chance to work with him or appreciate the qualities he has. When he moved me on to Livingston on loan, I played under Ray Stewart, but I've no idea if Ray was good, bad or indifferent as a manager, because I have little recollection of my time at the club. I was constantly drunk and full of cocaine.

I'd cleaned up my act by the time Bobby Williamson signed me for Kilmarnock. I enjoyed Bobby's training. He would play wee games and boxes, and we all got something out of it. He'd let the strikers go for crossing and finishing practice, and he'd take the defenders to work on their shape for the game at the weekend. He had the knack of keeping players happy, and there was rarely anybody in the dressing-room who had a bad word to say about Bobby or his backroom team of Gerry McCabe and Jim Clark. They never made anything complicated and always ensured that we were organised and ready to give 100 per cent.

When Jim Jefferies took over from Bobby, my first reaction to the news was, 'Fuck me, that's the fun over.' I just thought of Jim as being a dour, greeting-faced moaner. I'm glad to say my preconceptions were wrong. He only moaned half the time, and the other half he let Billy Brown do it for him!

I liked Jim and enjoyed his training. He and Billy were a great double act. It was the classic good-cop, bad-cop routine. Both have a great knowledge of the game, and I'd bet my last penny that any player who gets the chance to work under them will improve. Jim also has a terrific record in the transfer market. The way he works the system and sniffs out bargains is second to none. I'd love to see what he could do if he was given the chance to take charge of one of the Old Firm. Given the opportunity, I reckon he would be very successful.

Ian McCall took me back to Dundee United, and there's been no other manager I've worked under who liked a more competitive edge in training than he did. And most of the time, he'd be right in the thick of it. Ian would always play in the training games, and he hated losing. He was nippy when things weren't going his way, and he'd bend the rules to try and secure his team a win – or he'd just cheat and be blatant about it. The players hated it, and quite often both sides would end up kicking the shit out of each other. A few of the boys weren't comfortable with that, but I liked my training that way. The manager would be on the receiving end of a few tackles, and he dished it out too when he felt the need.

He also liked to have a 'Worst Player of the Week' award, and it was invariably me or Barry Robson who suffered the embarrassment of winning it. The punishment was to bring in cakes and juice for the rest of the team. I used to go to the best bakers in Dundee to make sure the boys were well looked after. I'd also buy bottles of Lucozade. In contrast, Craig Easton was the tightest guy in the world, and if he 'won' he'd go home and bake his own fairy cakes to save himself a tenner! I wouldn't have minded, but his home baking was minging. He'd also go to the local corner shop and buy a cheap bottle of diluting orange!

Dundee was Alex Rae's first job in management, and he made mistakes. He was trying to do too much and should have delegated more. He left the training to his assistant Davie Farrell, and the stuff we got day to day was good. Alex and I would sit down with a cup of tea and chat away about football and life in general. It was great therapy. He was keen to make sure the boys had good habits, and he also brought in psychologists to help us. Basically, he would do anything that would improve the players, help the team win on a Saturday and make the club as professional as possible. But he had a young squad and needed more experience. It was a pity he had to build his squad based on what players were earning rather than on ability. He wanted to keep a few players but had to let them go because of the wages they were on. Alex hates losing, and I reckon he will have a good future as a manager.

Alex was just one of a number of top-class managers I've worked with throughout my career. I didn't necessarily see eye to eye with all of them, but I'd like to think that I learned something from every one of them. And I'd also like to believe, despite my off-field problems, that I gave them something in return *on* the pitch.

18

THE FUTURE — NO MORE MR VICE GUY

I'M NOT even halfway through my life, but I've managed to pack in more in those first 34 years than most people go through in a lifetime. Abuse, suicide, death, drugs, drink, gambling, parenthood, rehabilitation, fame and infamy: you name it, I've gone through it. However, after coping with 34 years of everything that life's thrown at me, I'm still here. I'm lucky to have a beautiful family, lucky to be doing something that most guys can only dream of, and most of all lucky to have entered the middle years of my life stronger, happier and above all a better person for my experiences.

When I was a kid, I used to be scared of dying. Sometimes, I couldn't sleep at night for worrying about never waking up again. I don't know why I had that terrible fear. Maybe a lot of kids have it, I'm not sure. The thought of not seeing my family and friends again left me pretty distraught. When I think about it now, it seems silly.

Up until a few years ago, my main worry in life was what I was going to do once I stopped playing football. However, now that I'm down to the final two or three years of my career, I'm not concerned about it in the slightest. In fact, I'm relishing getting stuck into something different. I'm excited about what may lie ahead in the next few years. I really can't wait to go out into the world and find a 'real' job.

But that's the big question: what can I do when I leave

the comfort and sanctuary of the dressing-room. It's the only environment I've known as an adult. Many players struggle with their lives once they leave the game in their mid-30s. They have no decent education behind them, no one to take care of their needs and not enough money in the bank. But I've got experience behind me. Life experience. All those hours spent torturing myself and analysing my existence have taught me a thing or two about how to cope with the pitfalls of life. And I want to pass that knowledge onto other people, particularly teenage kids. The way your life develops has a lot to do with what happens in your teenage years. Stick in with your education, keep your head down and hang around with the right kind of people and your life should start on the right path. Skip school, start to bevvy and hang out with the wrong kind of people and you follow the path of self-destruction. It's a path I know only too well.

I'd particularly like to get involved with football clubs and advise their young professionals about the best way they can look after themselves off the park. Clubs should want to do everything in their power to protect their young players. After all, they are potentially worth millions in the transfer market, and the clubs shouldn't be allowed to ruin their investment through negligence.

We all know too much alcohol is bad for you, gambling to excess may well see your house being repossessed and taking drugs could leave you a wreck, but it's about going deeper than that. Why do I want to snort cocaine? Why do I want a drink first thing in the morning? Why have I been feeling like shit for the past two days? I genuinely believe that when I was starting my career as a footballer, I might not have ended up with the problems I had, had there been someone there to advise me about the potential problems and pitfalls. Someone like me.

Occasionally, as part of the YTS scheme, a guy would come in and speak to us about vices outside the game. To be honest, I never really paid any attention and had no interest in what he had to say. However, had he been a person with a proper footballing background, I would have sat up straight and taken on board every word. I'm not saying I disrespected the guy, but if our adviser had been an ex-pro, the chances of us heeding his advice would have been much higher. When it's an 'outsider', there is a mentality within the game that that person's intruding on our world. Football can be very insular.

Ross Mathie invited me down to Inverclyde a couple of years ago to speak to the Scotland Under-16 and Under-17 squads about the perils of alcohol and drugs. I was nervous about addressing these young international players, but once I started I felt really confident and received a lot of positive feedback. I was grateful to Ross, who is a lovely guy and a fine coach. There's something cathartic about talking your problems through with other people. Talking definitely helps the healing process.

Ross Mathie: I had a group of Scotland youth players for an international gathering, and part of their time with us was spent learning about different aspects of the game. We had a sports scientist in to speak to them, we gave them media training and we brought in an agent to speak to them about that side of the business.

There was also a slot for a chat on drugs awareness, and I thought Andy would be the perfect man to come and speak to the players. I think that this was in 2001, and Andy had not long played for the full Scotland side against Poland. I wrote to him at Kilmarnock, and within three days he was on the phone to me. 'Hi, Ross. Where and when do you want me to do this?' It was as straightforward as that.

Andy reported to Inverclyde, and he stood outside the lecture theatre while I was inside giving the boys the lowdown on who was coming to speak to them. I put on a video of Andy in action. It was the 1989 World Cup final at Hampden against Saudi Arabia. The match finished 2–2 and went to a penalty shoot-out. Andy took the third kick and scored. The footage showed him walking away, smoking an imaginary cigar. That was in front of a worldwide television audience and a packed national stadium. I then explained what had happened to him with drink and drugs, and that he had shown tremendous resilience to bounce back and play for Scotland against Poland.

Andy then entered the room, pulled up a chair, turned it round back to front and sat with his hands hanging over the edge to address the players. 'Hello,' he said. 'My name is Andy McLaren, and I'm an alcoholic.' You could have heard a pin drop. He had the full attention of the players and the Scotland backroom staff.

Andy spoke for around 30 minutes. He didn't have any notes – there was nothing prepared. He just spoke straight from the heart. His words had a resounding effect. He was magnificent, and it wasn't an easy audience, as it can be difficult to hold the full attention of youth players, especially when there are around 30 of them in the room. He chatted about how he nearly lost his family because of drink and drugs and how he wasted huge chunks of his career. He then threw it open to the floor and was comfortable taking questions from the players.

I've listened to many people address footballers, but Andy McLaren was by far the most impressive. His session was different class. Football clubs now do their own drugs-awareness programmes, so there isn't as much of a need for the SFA to do it when we have squad gatherings. But I know that I'd have every confidence in using Andy in the future.

I've known him for the best part of 20 years, as I coached him through the international youth ranks. He's always been a character, and he always had lots of talent as a footballer. I've total respect for Andy, and I wish him well in the next stage of his life.

I want to do more of that kind of thing. And I don't just want to speak to footballers. I'd like to speak to people in all walks of life. Receiving counselling from Peter Kay at Sporting Chance opened my eyes to the possibilities. Peter has helped the SPL by going to their member clubs to give talks, and he's asked me to tag along. I've not taken him up on the offer yet, but I probably will before too long.

At the moment, my plan would be to start working within an organisation that deals with counselling and therapy. I'd like to go in, establish the mechanics of how it all operates and offer my input. To this end, I attended a 12-week course at Glasgow's Langside College a few years ago called 'Introduction to Counselling'. I was a bit apprehensive about going along, but I actually enjoyed it. Quite a bit of what was taught on the course was stuff I'd picked up while being in the Priory and at AA gatherings. But one thing that was hammered home to me was the need to be a good listener. When people are in bother, they want to talk and get rid of the burden that's weighing them down. At the end of the day, 99 per cent of society knows right from wrong, but it is hard to admit out loud the mistakes you are making and the hurt and damage you are causing. Once you're able to do that, you are on the right road. But it is vital to have the right place to go to and the right person to talk to.

When I first admitted my alcoholism, it took me a long time to open up. I didn't feel comfortable sitting with a bunch of strangers discussing my personal problems. But once I got to know a few of them and started to feel at ease in their company, I was able to trust them, and I began to let things out, a little bit at a time.

There should be more avenues for people to find help and build a trusting relationship with someone. And it shouldn't cost thousands and thousands of pounds, either. Hopefully, if I can get involved in this line of work, then people will identify with my story and feel that they can approach me for a form of comfort or to sound off to – whatever they need to help them through their crisis. Trust is such an important part of it all, and I'd like to think that I'd be the type of person whom people would be able to speak to. I was so lucky to find Angela Maguire and Peter Kay.

Both have been excellent sounding boards for me and helped me to get on with things and see the positive side when life was dragging me down. They never ever put pressure on me, just allowed me to release my thoughts when I wanted to.

It disturbs me that there are thousands of people walking the streets who have been sexually abused and haven't been able to stand up to the problem. It took me long enough. If you are a victim, don't let it eat you up any longer. Find the right person and open up. I guarantee you will feel so much better about yourself if you share your feelings, and you can then start the healing process.

In time, starting up my own help group is something I'd like to do. I don't have the business acumen to do it, but if I can get involved with someone who has the expertise and suitable finances, then it could be a goer. I'd like to work with a couple of counsellors and have a helpline available 24 hours a day. It's something I know I can do, and I hope that it's an idea I can get off the ground in the not too distant future.

I have all this experience from stuff that's happened off the field, but on the pitch I've been there and done it, too: an international cap, cup finals, relegation, promotion and not forgetting a World Cup final! So, it's also in my thoughts to put that experience to good use. I'm thinking about gaining my coaching badges so that I can stay in football after I hang up my boots. I don't believe I'm cut out to be a manager, and having that pressure is not something that appeals to me, but I reckon I would be a good number two – a good link between the dressing-room and the manager's office. I like to believe that players would feel comfortable speaking to me and would be able to tell me if they were having a bad day. Talking about things is one of the best ways to get to the root of a problem. I never really had that kind of relationship with the coaching staff at my clubs. Of course, I was in a helluva state most of the time and in denial, so I wasn't exactly amenable to help.

As I reach the twilight of my career, I realise that I have to give something back, whether it's on or off the park. I have no idea what I'll be doing five years from now, but I pray life continues to improve for me and my family. The past few years have been so positive, and my only regret is that I didn't clean up my act much sooner.

Not long ago, I visited my mum's house with Dylan. We sat and had a cup of tea and a blether, then mum produced her collection of videos of my career – from the Under-16 World Cup to my days with Dundee United and Kilmarnock. In many of them, I was fresh-faced and full of running with a decent turn of pace, skill, an eye for goal and not a grey hair in sight. I didn't recognise myself! Dylan didn't, either. It was lovely to sit and watch them all and share that afternoon with my son. I've never been one to reminisce and brag about the old days, but I enjoyed my trip down memory lane that afternoon. I sat there and watched a few of the games over and over again. I could have stayed there for a month. God bless Mum for keeping them.

At the end of the day, Dylan turned to me and said, 'Dad, you really were some player. Why didn't you make more of your career?' What could I say to that? Dylan meant well and was really proud to have seen me in action, but I knew why he'd asked. I also knew the answer: I made a total mess of it. I can't blame any other person for my self-destruction.

Writing this book has been so good for me, because it's made me analyse my life, talk, cringe, cry and have a few laughs along the way. It's been good fun, and doing the research on the early part of my career brought back so many memories: the people I've worked with; the players I've shared dressing-rooms with; the managers who could take no more of my antics and lack of professionalism. Many of the people whom I've asked to recall memories of me have been tremendously warm. That has been a source of so much encouragement. Deep down, they knew I wasn't a bad guy. I was just messed up and couldn't get out of the situation I was in.

Doing the autobiography has also been a fantastic help with my ongoing rehabilitation. The pages of this book are like one long confession. However, parts have not been easy to write, and I have often doubted whether I was doing the right thing by revealing so much about what has happened in my life. One day, I'd be up for it and would spill out all the details; the next day, I'd want to run a million miles from it all. Indeed, there were days, weeks even, when I did run away and was sick of talking about my life. It was my way of dealing with things, and my way of soul-searching to find out what I really wanted to write about it. Writing about being abused as a child was particularly painful, but I wanted to go through the pain to emerge on the other side a stronger person. I hope my honesty leads to someone else feeling they can also open up and realising that they are not alone.

What I have to do now is make sure ten years from now I am not sitting here with regrets about what I've done or not managed to do in the past decade. I'm about to enter a new chapter in my life. Yes, I'm a little apprehensive about what lies ahead, but I know with the love of my family and my support network around me I can make a success of the next ten years. It won't be easy. Each day is a battle, and, like every person out there, I will have my good days and bad days. But I'm ready to face it all. Ready for anything that comes my way. Ready to be proud of myself. And ready to make my family proud of me.